Tools and Materials

FOR CALLIGRAPHY

ILLUMINATION AND MINIATURE PAINTING

Patricia Lovett

C Roberson and Co Ltd

British Library Cataloguing in Publication Data

A catalogue record for this book is available from the British Library

ISBN 0 9529387 0 7

Published by C Roberson and Co Ltd, 105 Great Russell Street, London WC1B 3RY.
Telephone: *0171·272·0567 0171·636·1045*
Designed by Hernewood Studio, Sevenoaks, Kent.
Printed and bound by The Caxton and Holmesdale Press Ltd., Sevenoaks, Kent.

Contents

About the author

Patricia Lovett is a professional scribe whose work often involves raised gilding and painting on vellum. She regularly exhibits pieces in the UK and abroad.

Patricia studied at Reigate College of Art for the HSDAD in Art and Design specialising in Calligraphy, Heraldry and Illumination, which covered many of the skills of the mediæval scribe. Since then she has taught lettering to adults and children for more years than she would care to remember, specialising in the less familiar alphabet styles and expressive calligraphy as well as the scribe's traditional skills. She initiated and teaches the ***Calligraphy and Lettering Arts Society*** Gilding and Traditional Skills Certificate Course.

Because of her interest in education, children and young people Patricia founded and runs **L E T T E R S,** which is a society for those interested in all forms of letters and lettering.

Her other books on lettering include *Teach Yourself Calligraphy, Calligraphy for Starters, Creating Letterforms* and *Starting Lettering,* the last two being co-written. She has also made a video, *Calligraphy for Starters,* for beginners and improvers.

Patricia is Youth Officer for the *Calligraphy and Lettering Arts Society* and Calligraphy Officer for *Alphabugs.* She is a Fellow of CLAS and the RSA.

Acknowledgments:

Teaching is always a learning process. Much of what is in this book has come about because students have asked 'why?', 'is that always the case?' and 'but what if...?' about subjects and matters which I thought initially were fairly straightforward. I am indebted to all those 'but what if ...?' students because they have made me question and find out information for myself as well as for them.

Nicholas Walt, proprietor of C Roberson and Co Ltd, London, was the main driving force behind the production of this book. It was his idea to go ahead with an informative volume of this sort. Thanks are also due to Jacqueline Conning who has kept me sane over the past few months, and to the un-named proof reader, who knows who he is, and how much his corrections and amendments are appreciated!

And of course, my family, whose patience and forbearance, yet unfailing support at all times, have been a great strength.

Introduction

English painting and lettering in the manuscript books of mediæval times exemplify the excellence of the artist, illuminator and scribe. Although there has been a number of occasions since these books were produced when the skills required for producing them were thought redundant, there have always been a number of artists and enthusiasts of these crafts to ensure their continuity.

During the last century many of the skills associated with lettering with a broad edge nib and illuminating had been forgotten. It was William Morris (1834 – 1896) and the rise of the Arts and Crafts movement which led to a new study of calligraphy and gilding. Morris's daughter, May, remembers many sheets of paper in her father's study, lying around for a number of years, covered with his experiments using different types of raising compound, and his studies of recipes of these from old books. The evidence from his own hand-written and illuminated manuscript books shows that Morris was successful, but it was Edward Johnston (1872 – 1944) and his associates and students who, at the beginning of this century, made the most progress in rediscovering the techniques and skills of manuscript work. Their task was not easy. Many of the original materials were no longer available, and modern substitutes had not yet been produced.

And now, after a period of time when interest in letters and lettering has again been in decline for a number of years, there are many people who want to know more about writing in a calligraphic style and how to illuminate and paint manuscripts. Yet what tools and materials do they, should they use? The inks and paints, gold, brushes, burnishers and papers required for these interests are specialised and yet it is not easy to find out what is the best or most appropriate, even from specialist shops. This book has been written specifically for these people who may be beginners, improvers, or those who have spent some years in some aspects of the crafts but who may be unfamiliar with the full range of materials which can be used.

Someone new to calligraphy or miniature painting, standing in the middle of an art shop or specialist suppliers, may well be daunted by the wealth of choice on offer – inks of all kinds, liquid and stick – watercolour and oil paints – gouache and poster paints – golds of all types from the cheapest gouache to the most expensive fine illuminating gold leaf. And then there are all these gums and glues, powders and potions. What are they all used for and are they all needed? And in addition to all this are brushes and burnishers, papers and vellum.

To help to prevent confusion, there are chapters on all of these topics in this book. It is not specifically a 'how to' book for writing – you will not find guidelines on how to write different alphabets here – what you will find is information about pens and inks, paints, brushes and papers. You will also find brief guidelines on how to use the various media for lettering and painting and also details on areas of the craft, such as egg tempera painting, which are rarely covered in other books.

Essentially this book is a reference and was written to be of use to the specialist and non-specialist alike.

Pens, Brushes, Burnishers and Other Tools

For calligraphy, as with so many other arts and crafts, it is ideal if you can buy the best quality equipment that you can afford and which is suited to the purpose. The important point is to avoid making expensive purchases which are not worthwhile. This chapter is to help you decide what is best for what you want to do.

Pens

There are different types of calligraphy pens – felt tip pens, fountain pens and 'dip' pens. All of these have a tip which emulates or is a broad edge nib. This is what makes the thicks and thins in calligraphic letters. The only exception to this is the Copperplate nib, which is dealt with in its own section.

It should perhaps be pointed out that right-handers should choose nibs which are straight cut and left-handers, left-oblique nibs.

These different pens all have advantages and disadvantages and are suited to different purposes. You should decide what you want the pen for before you make your purchase.

Calligraphy felt tip pens

These are available in a limited range of widths and colours. They are very easy to use and transport, and are ideal for beginners or for working out roughs. They are disposable, however, and do not last forever, nor can they be refilled. Their tips are not particularly fine, and the letters they produce do not have very crisp thicks and thins. Their limited width and colour range also means that you are therefore limited in the colour of and size of letters you produce. However, most professional scribes will have felt-tip pens in their pen pots for easy practice or for working out ideas.

At present, few ranges of calligraphic felt tip pens are available in left-oblique tips for left-handers.

Calligraphy fountain pens

The ranges of nib widths and colour of inks for calligraphy fountain pens are similar to those for felt tip pens. However, the end of the nib is finer and thus the letters produced are that much crisper.

Fountain pens are often used by beginners as well as those with a little experience. They are easily transportable and are ideal for practice, as there are no palettes of paint to worry about.

The nib of the fountain pen can be a little rigid as it is manufactured to remain in close contact with the feeding mechanism. If it was very flexible there would not be a consistent flow of ink as the nib is moved to and fro from the ink supply. However, some pen manufacturers have responded to this problem of a rigid nib and are now making fountain pens which produce very good letters. Whether a fountain pen will ever be produced which has as flexible a nib as a dip pen is debatable.

Most manufacturers of calligraphy fountain pens produce them with left-oblique nibs for left handers.

The nibs for fountain pens can usually be sharpened to make the writing edge finer and more flexible. For sharpening nibs see page 16.

Always use the fountain pen ink manufactured for that pen, and look for an ink that is not too watery.

Calligraphy dip pens

Apart from quills, calligraphy dip pens produce the sharpest and crispest letters. The nibs are manufactured to be flexible and responsive. They can also be sharpened to make letterforms even better, see page 16. Dip pen nibs are produced in a range of sizes, sometimes as many as ten different widths of nibs in one range and they are manufactured in a left-oblique range, too, for left-handers.

Most dip pen sets are sold as a separate pen holder, range of nibs and reservoirs. Sometimes the reservoirs are attached to the pen holder, or they may be part of the nib itself. When assembling the pen, make sure that the reservoir is about 2 – 3mm ($^{1}/_{8}$ inch) below the tip of the nib. It should touch the nib, but not be so tight that the nib is squeezed by the sides, or the two sides of the nib will be pressed apart. The reservoirs are very flexible. Bend your reservoir until it is in the correct position and not straining the nib at any point.

When beginning calligraphy, choose a wide nib. This will show your letterforms up to best effect. As time goes on you can use nibs which are narrower, and your writing will then be smaller.

Although they are called dip pens, it is best not to dip the nib into ink or paint. If you do so there is usually a blob of liquid on top of the nib which will flood the first stroke you write. It is better to use an old brush to feed the ink or paint into the nib by stroking it along the side or the top of the nib. This liquid will collect between the nib and the reservoir and be ready for when you write. Alternatively, if you feel you must dip, then have a piece of rag handy to wipe the top of the nib clean.

Start a dip pen nib by going backwards and forwards making a very narrow stroke. When the ink is flowing well you can then make thicker strokes.

Beginners are often frustrated by dip pens not writing easily. This may be caused by one of two factors. First, they sometimes do not realise how often a pen needs to be filled. Wide nibs, making letters where the x-height is 1·5cm, or half-an-inch, often need to be filled for every stroke or letter. As well as this, beginners may fill their pen, look at the letter to be copied, look again, find the place along a line, and then start to write. In so doing, the ink has dried at the edge of the nib and the pen will not write. Go back and forwards making those narrow strokes if this happens to you, and as soon as the pen starts to write well, then make your letter without hesitation or checking. If you continue to have problems, the ink or paint may be too thick. Add a little water to dilute it. When you are comfortable with your writing you can use the more viscous ink.

You can write with calligraphy inks, see page 29, or gouache, see page 34, with calligraphy dip pens. This means that you can write in any colour, shade or tone that you wish. With the range of nib widths that there are your choices of lettering size and colour are almost endless.

Quills

Quills are feathers which have been treated and shaped so that they can be used as pens. Art shops and specialist suppliers often have feathers from geese, turkeys or swans, all of which are suitable for quills. Swan feathers have the longest and widest barrels; turkey feathers are often the strongest, but the barrels are relatively short; goose feathers are narrow, but the barrels are quite long.

The first five flight feathers are suitable for quills, but the first and second are best as the barrels are longest. Feathers do not have to be

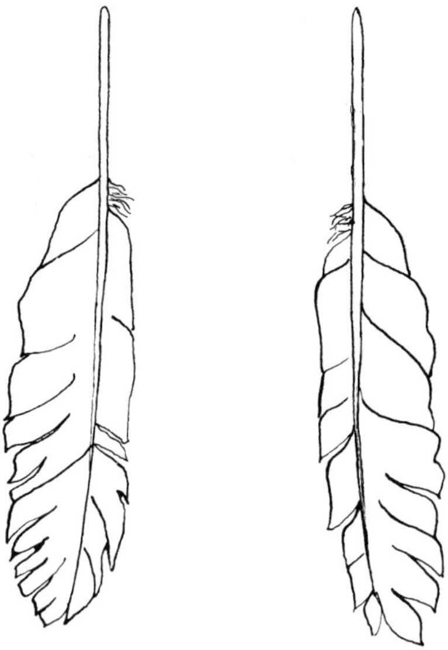

As the feathers curve around the bird's body, right-handers should choose feather from the left wing, and left-handers feathers from the right wing. This means that the cut quills will curve away from the scribe's body in use.

Feathers for left-handers, *and right-handers.*

pulled from the birds, they are simply picked up from the ground during the moulting season. Because of the curved shape of the bird's body, those from the left wing are best for right-handers, and those from the right wing for left-handers.

If kept for long enough the feathers will dry out and harden naturally. However, it is usually preferable to help the hardening process on its way by firing the feathers for a few seconds in a dish of hot fine sand; the feathers should have been previously been soaked in water and the rounded tip cut off. Alternatively you can use a warm domestic iron and make a dutching tool from a handle and brass cup hook. Heat the dutching tool on the iron, place it inside the barrel and then rotate the feather on the iron. The opaque feather should be heated until it becomes clear and goes slightly yellow; it should be very hard. Unlike the feathers soaked in water which are very pliable, you should not be able to squeeze the sides of a hardened quill together without breaking them.

Clean the outside of the feather by scraping it with your fingernail or the back of the blade of a pair of scissors. Pull out the inner membrane with a crochet hook. Cut off the feathery top of the feather until it is about 20cm, 8 inches, long. Remove any of the remaining barbs.

Using a curved bladed knife, cut the shape of a pen nib at the end of the feather. Make a long 2cm scoop cut on the underneath of the feather, going half way through the diameter of the barrel. Now shape the shoulders of the nib by making two side cuts; halfway along that first cut, about 1cm from the tip, make a cut on one side which curves in and then goes straight towards the tip. Rest the knife where you started to make this first cut and rotate the quill slightly to make the second cut. This should then match the first. You will now see the nib shape forming.

You can make a dutching tool by straightening out a brass cup hook and inserting it in a wooden handle for ease of use. The dutching tool is used to harden or clarify feathers to make quills.

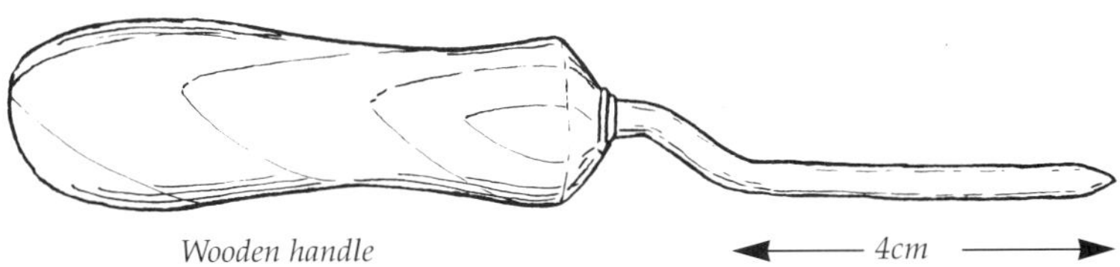

Cut a slit for the nib to work properly. Rest the quill on a surface such as a cutting mat, and make a tiny slit in the middle of the 'nib' which you have cut. Use the end of a paintbrush as a lever to extend the slit. Place your thumbnail at the point where you want to slit to end.

All that remains now is to trim the tip. Left-handers can make a left-oblique nib at this point. Resting the quill on a cutting mat, concentrate on the very end. Using the curved part of the blade, cut about 0·5cm, a quarter of an inch, from the nib tip. Now make a bevel cut at the very end, and lastly, cut one tiny sliver from the very tip of the nib.

Cutting a quill.

Make a long scoop cut on the underside of the quill, going through about half the diameter of the barrel.

Shape the shoulders by making two scoop cuts on the top of the feather – they should go in and then straight along towards the end.

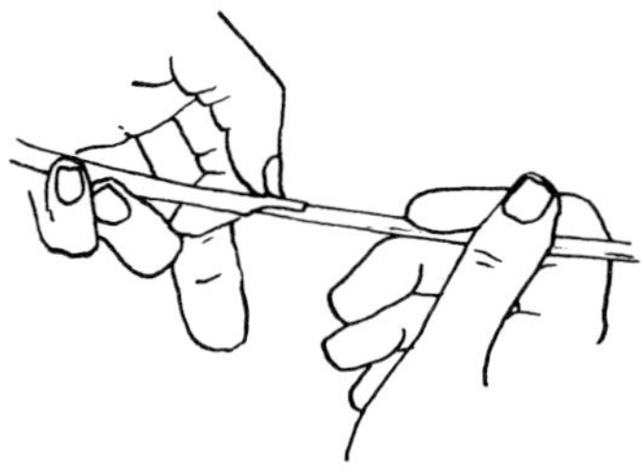

Make a little slit with the knife and increase this with the end of a paintbrush used as a lever. Place your thumbnail where you want the slit to end.

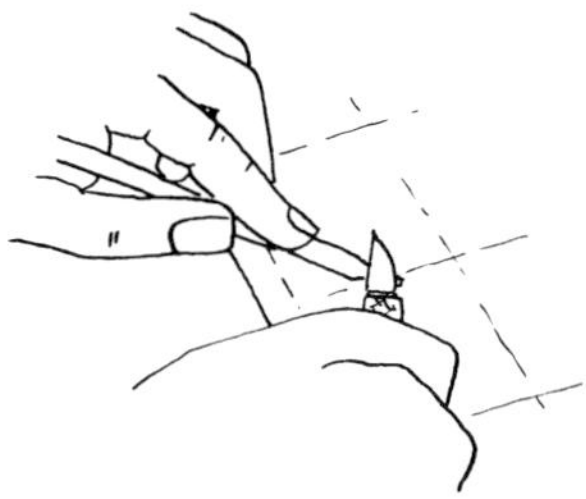

Cut about 0·5cm off the very end, and then cut a bevel. Lastly cut a tiny sliver from the very tip.

You will need to sharpen the nib when you are using it, by taking the tiniest straight cut from the end. At some point you will need to recut the bevel as well as trimming the end.

The quill will last as long as the barrel. If quills are allowed to dry out the two sides may well separate. Before using, wrap the ends of the quill in a piece of damp paper kitchen roll or a wet tissue. This will bring the two ends together again within an hour or two.

Copperplate nibs

Copperplate nibs are different from other calligraphy pens and nibs because they are pointed. They also cannot be sharpened and can lose their spring, and so you will need many more of these nibs than broad edge ones.

Copperplate nibs are very flexible, and there are no specific sizes. You use one nib to write most sizes of letters simply by pressing harder when writing larger letters. Their very flexibility means that you do not use a reservoir with Copperplate nibs, and so will need to refill your pen quite frequently.

Some Copperplate nibs are manufactured with an elbow shape, and sometimes pen holders are elbow shaped, too. As the paper for Copperplate writing is held at quite an angle with the left-hand corner much lower than the right (for all other styles it is best if the paper is held straight), this elbow shape does help some, but not all, scribes. Left-handers may prefer to have their paper upright.

Brushes

Calligraphic letters can be written with any brush – a broad edge brush to match broad edge nib letters, or pointed for Copperplate-type letters. Any brush can be used – even a home decorating brush will give reasonable, if rather spiky, letters.

You may prefer a more conventional type of brush available from most art shops, though. Brushes which are similar to a broad edge nib are called one-stroke brushes. For lettering you do not necessarily need a brush made with natural hair. One manufactured from nylon or similar synthetic material is usually sufficient.

For miniature painting and painted letters with fine lines, a pointed brush is preferable. As with other tools, there are various qualities available.

Brushes are manufactured with different shaped holders and with different quality hairs. The very best hairs for brushes are those made with Kolinksy sable. To be more specific, the hairs from the tail of the winter coat of the male sable. However, this is rarely specified on the narrow wooden brush handle! It is quite difficult to find true Kolinksy sable brushes nowadays, but the extra spring in these brushes makes them well worth searching out. Other sable brushes are also good, and if you cannot get real sable, then the very best quality of synthetic brush would be acceptable.

For miniature painting or painting fine lettering the brushes used are so small that Kolinsky sable brushes are not prohibitively expensive. The sizes needed are 000 and 00. Larger areas of colour or larger letters can be painted with a size 1 brush.

Choosing a brush

Usually art shops have a container of brushes on their counter, or they may have brushes still in their packets in drawers. Select one brush, dampen the end of your finger (there will normally be a jug of water to hand) and roll the point of the brush on this. Hold the brush up to the light. The brush should come to a good, even point, without any stray hairs sticking out. These will ruin your painting, especially of fine lines, and although they can be cut off with a sharp knife, this ruins the balance of the hairs and the shape of the brush.

Burnishers

When working with fine gold, you will need a burnisher to bring up a real mirror shine without damaging the surface of the gold leaf. Burnishers are made from polished stone or metal ore, and there are various shapes and sizes.

For illuminating, the very large sized burnishers are not required. We need a size and shape to manipulate easily around the cushion

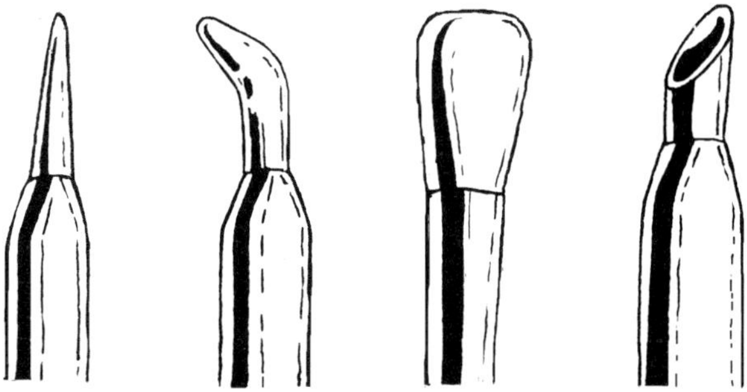

Burnishers come in different shapes and sizes: from the left – pencil-shaped, dog-tooth, spade-shaped and lipstick-shaped.

of gesso, so something which tucks the gold leaf into the edge, as well as being able to polish over an area of gold which may be 3 or 4cm wide, is necessary.

Burnishers are available in different shapes – dog-tooth, pencil-, spade- and lipstick-shaped. It depends on your personal preference which one you should choose. I have always used a dog-tooth shape, with a diameter of about 3mm, and prefer this for all my gilding. I find that I can use the rounded tip and the curve of the burnisher to tuck in gold and polish larger areas. Some other illuminators prefer lipstick-shapes. You may choose also to have a pencil-shaped burnisher. With this you can push patterns into the polished gold.

The cheapest burnishers are made of polished agate, and I have used an agate burnisher successfully for many years. It gives a cold burnish. Some burnishers are made of psilomelanite; this is a manganese ore, and usually these burnishers are lipstick-shaped. The most expensive burnishers are polished hæmatite; only this type of burnisher gives a hot burnish, and seem to help to almost weld the gold to the gesso. They are best used for the final polishing of the gold, when some pressure is required.

Other tools

There are other tools, apart from pens, brushes and burnishers which will make your work as a scribe that much easier.

Sharpening Stone

The best letterforms are made with a pen which has a fine, sharp nib. Even new pen nibs are not always as sharp as they could be. Sharpening nibs reduces very slightly the metal on the top edge of the nib, thus making it more flexible.

Sharpening a nib is not difficult but you will require a sharpening stone. The best are made from fine-grade Arkansas stone, available from specialist suppliers. You can also use the smoother side of an India sharpening stone, but the finer the grade of stone, the sharper your nib will be.

Make sure that the end of the nib is straight by going backwards and forwards along that edge on the sharpening stone 7 or 8 times. Now sharpen the upper side of the nib, just at the tip. Turn the nib over so that the upper edge is on the stone, and, at an angle of about 30° for wide nibs and 20° for narrow nibs, stroke the nib on the stone about 7 or 8 times. You should be able to see a shiny metal strip at the end of the nib when you have sharpened well.

The process of sharpening may have caused a few metal burs on the nib. Remove these by stroking the side corners and the underneath of the nib on the stone once or twice. Your nib should be sharp

Sharpening nibs.

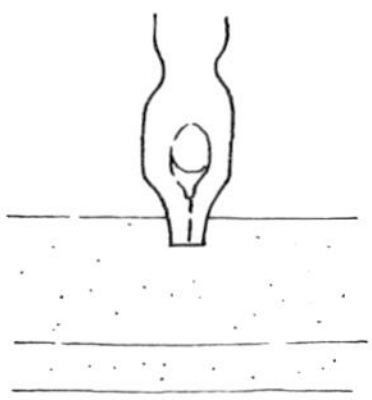

Straighten the end of the nib first, by stroking this on the stone 7 or 8 times.

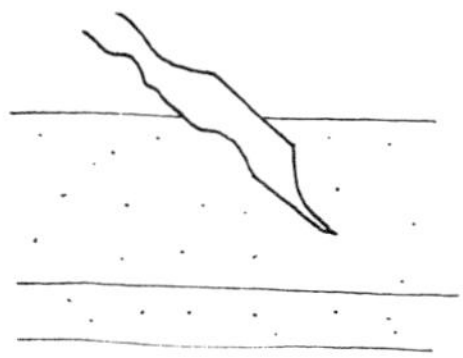

Now sharpen the top edge of the nib by stroking it 7 or 8 times.

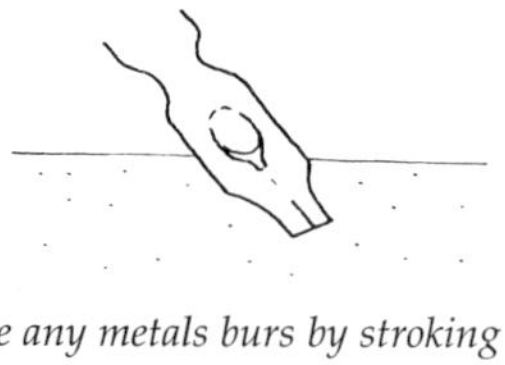

Remove any metals burs by stroking the side corners a couple of times,

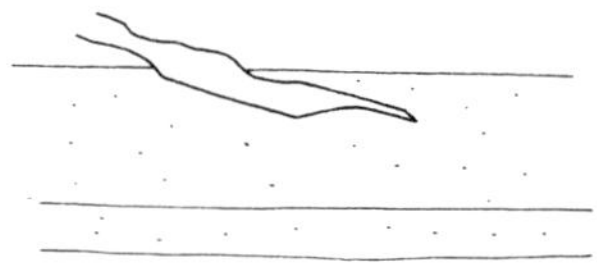

and then the underneath. The top edge of your nib should be shiny metal.

enough to write very crisp letters but not so sharp that it cuts the paper. If this is the case, dull the nib by stroking the end a couple of times on the stone, in the same way as you straightened it.

Knives

You will need two types of knives for calligraphy and gilding. One simply cuts and trims paper and sharpens pencils, so any sharp bladed knife is suitable. Disposable ones are good as they are cheap. However, you may prefer a more substantial knife where the blade can be sharpened, or one where the blades can be replaced.

For cutting quills and dealing with gesso, you will need a knife with a curved blade. Scalpels are not really substantial enough for quill cutting. You want a knife with a solid handle which will not twist in your hand. The ones I prefer are those which have interchangeable blades. They are usually sold complete with a normal knife blade, and curved blades can be bought separately, often in little containers of five. As it is easy to change the blades, normally by simply turning the knurled part of the handle, you can economise by having one handle and separate straight blades and curved blades – although the ones for cutting quills and scraping gesso should be stored separately and the containers clearly marked.

Pencils

It is important for accurate lettering that the lines you draw should be straight and fine. The best pencils for this are ones which retain their point for a long time. Soft pencils – HB and all the B range – do not do this and also tend to smudge and make your work dirty. Although it may take you a little time to get used to them as the lines they draw are faint, choose pencils which are at least 2H and preferably 4H. Use a knife rather than a pencil sharpener to maintain a long, sharp point, and re-sharpen often.

When drawing lines use the longest ruler you can get hold of, especially if your paper is wide. A T-square or set square is better. Make sure that the angle you hold your pencil is the same along the line you are drawing. If you change this angle the lines become closer together or further away, and this then alters the x-height of the letters you will write.

A set of dividers

It is much easier and quicker in measuring out the width of lines for your letters to use a set of dividers, or two sets. Dividers are similar to a set of compasses, but have two points rather than a pencil and point at the ends of the arms. It is not necessary to buy expensive dividers unless you choose to do so. Most sets of reasonable, cheap compasses are sold with a spare point as well as spare pencil leads. Remove the pencil from one end of the compasses and replace this with the spare point, thus creating a set of dividers. If possible, choose a set which has a knurled wheel for altering the distance between the arms. This means that whenever you put the dividers down you will not lose the accurate distance between them.

Two sets of dividers means that you can measure the preferred distance between lines with one set. 'Walk' this down one edge of your paper. You will have a set of pin pricks which mark your measurements. Now use the second set of compasses to mark out the width of lines for the x-height. If you need to draw additional lines, these compasses retain these measurements accurately.

If your work is not being framed simply trim off the edge with the pin pricks using a metal straight edge and sharp knife.

Sloping board

You should write at a sloping board as this controls the flow of ink from your pen as well as making a writing session much more comfortable. You can make your own sloping board by using a piece of board and propping it up with heavy books on a table. A proper designer's board, perhaps with an adjustable back and a sliding rule will make life very much easier. Choose the largest you can afford and accommodate, and cover the top with two flat sheets of white blotting paper to make a sympathetic writing surface.

Paper, Vellum and Other Surfaces

The range of papers available in most artshops can be bewildering. There is so much choice and variety but what sheets are suitable for calligraphy? And then there are skins, which is best – parchment, goatskin, vellum; and of vellum – manuscript, classic or bookbinder's?

Paper

The choices of paper for calligraphers are not so great as for watercolour artists. Most of the papers we want are smooth and with a tooth or edge to the paper so that the letters we write are sharp and crisp.

Paper for beginning lettering

When beginning calligraphy it is best to choose the cheapest paper that is reasonable to use. You will cover vast numbers of sheets with large letters, and it is not worth paying out large sums of money for expensive papers. Pads of A2 or A3 Layout Paper are usually recommended, although it is worth asking others what make of paper they use. Manufacturers have a habit of changing the quality of Layout Paper, which may be acceptable for other artists, but causes problems for scribes, as the letters may then be fuzzy and not crisp. Choosing a pad which is A2 is a good economy as you can always fold and cut the sheets in half if they are too large for your board. It does mean, however, that you have large sheets available when you want to do a larger piece, or when you want to make a paste-up for a large piece.

Some photocopying paper is also suitable for calligraphic use. Again choose the larger size, A3, if you can, as otherwise you will spend most of your practice time drawing guidelines. A ream of suitable A3 is a good investment for scribes, although do check that the paper works well with a pen before buying.

Computer paper often has a good 'tooth' to it, which calligraphers like for practice because some lines are very often drawn on the paper already, and this saves time.

Rolls of unpasted wallpaper and lining paper are useful for large letters, but the surface is too rough for using a calligraphic dip pen, unless you want a broken letter effect.

When doing a lot of practice, draw your guidelines in a fine black pen on a sheet of paper the same size as that you are using, and place this underneath Layout Paper or photocopying paper. You can usually see the lines easily underneath, and this will save you time.

Paper for best pieces

Paper is manufactured in different sizes and grain direction, weights and surface textures. What effect you want will determine your choice.

Paper size and grain direction

Most paper is now manufactured to standard size. The page size used for this book is about A5 (with some trimming). Two pages, opened out, will be A4 – 297mm by 210mm. This is the size of most photocopying paper. By doubling the shortest side each time the paper size increases from A10, being very small indeed to A0, which is very large!

Grain direction does not matter if you are using a whole sheet of paper, or cutting it. It does matter if you are folding it, perhaps to use in a book, or tearing it. All manufactured paper has grain direction, only hand-made paper does not. You will already have encountered grain direction if you have torn a coupon or article from a newspaper. One side is easy to tear, the other usually ends up with a ragged

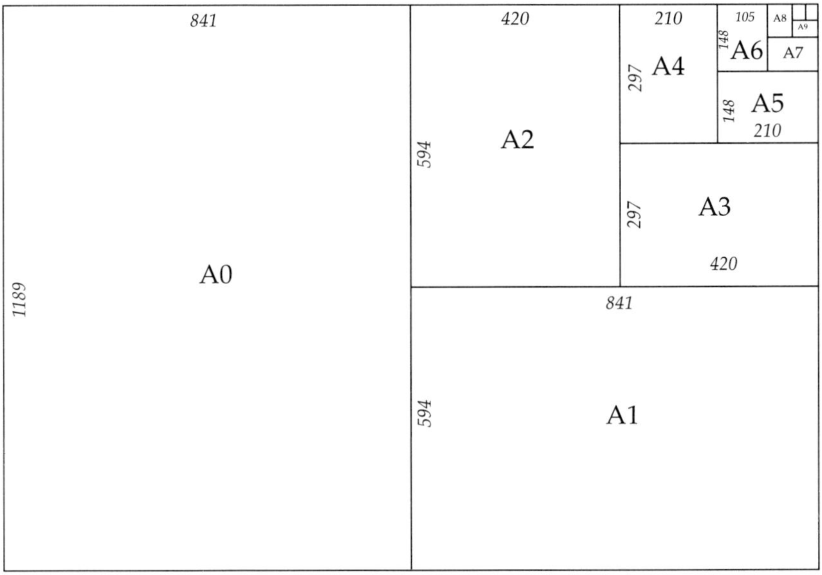

Standard paper sizes – all measurements in mm.

edge. It is easier to fold and tear paper along the grain direction.

You can find out grain direction in three main ways. First, gently bend a whole sheet of paper over one way, and then another. It will bend much more easily one way, and may even stay in that position. It will resist the other way and spring back. Secondly take a short length between the thumbs and forefingers of both hands, say about 10cm or 4 inches, along one side of the paper. Bend it gently between your hands. Now take a similar length along the side of the paper at right angles to the first. One side will bend more easily than the other. Or you could moisten a corner of the paper, say about 5cm or 2 inches in both directions. After a few seconds the paper will start to curl. The direction of the curl will indicate the grain direction.

Mark the grain direction with an arrow on your paper, and always fold it in this same direction.

Weight of paper

Paper used to be sold in weights according to the size of the sheet, so unless you knew that, you would not know how heavy or substantial the paper was. Now the weight of paper has been standardised, and it is sold according to the weight per square metre, this is called grammes per square metre, gsm or gm^2. The weight of paper used in this book is 100gsm, photocopying paper is 75 – 80gsm, reasonable quality calligraphy paper would be about 150gsm, something more robust between 250 – 350gsm, is getting towards a card weight.

The choice of weight of paper depends on what you want it for. In a manuscript book, paper which is between 150 – 180gsm would be best. Too heavy and the book becomes too bulky, too light and there is often show-through. Lighter weight papers can also be used for small pieces which will be framed fairly soon after you have finished them. Larger pieces, those which will not be framed, or those which will be handled a lot (such as a certificate or panel which will be signed by three or four people), should be in a paper which is heavier weight. Paper creases very easily, especially when handled carelessly, but if the paper is more robust it will stand up to this. I use paper which is 280 – 350gsm for panels and certificates, as it will not crease so easily before being presented. Paper of this weight also rolls well if being given in the form of a scroll. For this, grain direction should be taken into account again, as the paper should be rolled with the grain direction upright or vertical. Rolling against the grain is difficult.

Surface texture

Paper is made with one of three different surface textures. After manufacture the paper may be passed through heavy heated rollers. This produces paper with a smooth surface, such as that for this book, photocopying paper or letter writing paper. This paper is called *Hot Press* or *HP.* It is ideal for calligraphy as your letters will then be smooth and crisp.

If the paper is passed through cold rollers the surface is not so smooth. This paper is called *Not,* because it is not passed through hot rollers. In the USA this paper is called *Cold Press.* Letters on this paper will be more broken, but this can give an interesting effect.

Paper which still has the imprint of the textured felt which supported it when it was being made has a very rough texture, and is called *Rough.* Lettering on rough paper is much more broken and uneven.

Choosing paper
Your choice of a paper will depend on the purpose and should include weight, grain direction, surface texture and size. It may also include colour. Some pieces are best written out on a white or cream paper. This makes them look grand and elegant. Others may look best on a colour. There are many coloured papers which are good for lettering; do not think that calligraphy can only be written on plain papers.

Papers to look out for include the following, which have all been found to be suitable in their various ways for calligraphy, although it should be pointed out that this list is not exclusive:

White or cream papers
FABRIANO 5 *a white, smooth paper*
SAUNDERS WATERFORD *an off-white robust paper*
ARCHES AQUARELLE HP *a very smooth, off-white paper*
BOCKINGFORD *a slightly textured surface*
LAVIS FIDELIS *a good weight paper with different sides, one smoother and one more textured*
FABRIANO ROMA *an expensive hand-made paper*
RIVES BFK *paper for print-makers, but suitable for calligraphy if you have a light touch*
SOMERSET SATIN *paper, as its name suggests, with a satiny texture*
CANSON MI TEINTES *in white and cream with a texture to one side*
ZERKALL *a slightly textured paper available in pale tints*
VELIN PUR FIL JOHANNOT *a slightly textured paper*

Coloured papers
CANSON MI TEINTES *a good range of colours, one side is slightly textured*
FABRIANO INGRES *large sheets of a good range of colours*
KHADI *papers hand-made from India. The surface does not look as if it would be good for calligraphy, but it is!*
TRE KRONOR *paper with a ridged effect surface, but good and smooth for writing*

Paper Storage
Try to store your sheets of paper flat. It will then be ready to use when you want it. If you are limited for space, then wrap the paper

carefully, place it on a sheet of strong cardboard, or even plywood or MDF, and then slide it under the bed. Paper can be stored rolled, but you should roll it as loosely as you can, perhaps around a 10cm or 4 inch diameter 1 metre length of clean plastic drainpipe. You should roll it the other way very carefully, and then let it relax for 24 hours before you use it.

Crystal Parchment paper or glassine

This is a coated non-stick paper which is used not for writing, but in illuminating. Its special surface means that gold does not stick to it. This means that the gold can be pressed down on gesso or other adhesive with a burnisher without the leaves of gold adhering to the crystal parchment paper. It is available from specialist suppliers. If you have difficulty in obtaining sheets of crystal parchment paper then you can slit open the special glassine bags used by photographers to store and transport photographs.

Skins

Animal skins have been used for over 2,000 years as a surface for lettering and painting. That they have lasted for so long is testament to their ideal qualities for calligraphers. The surface is smooth and fine, and, when prepared properly, there is nothing better.

Vellum and parchment are the most common types of skin. There are a number of others but not all of them suitable for calligraphy.

Vellum is calfskin, although it is often called parchment, and parchment, which is sheepskin, is often called vellum!

Calfskin is the best surface for writing, and there are different qualities of this. The skins are prepared by soaking them in lime for a number of days. This removes much of the unwanted matter. When ready, the skins are stretched out on wooden frames. Small smooth pebbles are pushed through from underneath the skin; this gives a purchase for thongs, which are attached to wooden pegs on the frame. The thongs are wound round the pebbles and then the wooden pegs turned so that the skin is stretched until it is taut. The skins are scraped clean by very skilled parchmenters, using a semi-circular sharp blade, called a lunar knife. Shaving the skins in this way also reduced their thickness. Determining the point at which the skin is thin enough for use, without sticking the knife into the skin and thus damaging it, is a highly skilled job. Throughout the process, water is used as a lubricant. The skins are also treated with chalk, which acts as a de-greaser.

When the skins are ready they are cut from the wooden frame and rolled for storage and this is how the skins are sent out. Skins are very strong and tough and it is often a problem to remove the curl in the skin if it has been stored for some time in this way. If at all possible, store the skins flat. They will then be ready for you to use when you wish. If you cannot store them flat allow at least 24 hours for the skins to be rolled back carefully against the way in which they were stored, and allow them to relax so that they can be handled effectively.

Calfskin manuscript vellum

This is the best quality for calligraphy. It is prepared for writing on both sides, although if you have the choice, it is better to use the hair side only.

Vellum has the two sides you would expect from a natural skin – flesh and hair. The way to determine the difference is by look and feel. Feel both sides of vellum with your thumb; one side will feel smooth and the other slightly rough. Look carefully at the smooth side; it will probably look whiter and even a little waxy. The rougher side may have some of the markings of the skin, and be creamy or even beige or greenish in colour. The side which looks as though it should be used for writing – whiter, smooth and waxy – is the flesh side. The side which is rougher, coarser and more marked is the hair side, and the side much preferred for writing and painting. Therefore the hair side is that which should be used.

Classic vellum

Classic vellum is more marked than manuscript vellum; it is usually thicker. Classic vellum is prepared on only one side – the hair side –

and this is the side which should be used. Classic vellum is a wonderful surface for pieces which need some character in the writing surface.

Slunk vellum

This is very thin, fine vellum. It is traditionally from still-born or new-born calves. However, mostly it is the parchmenter's skill which has produced these fine, almost transparent, skins by scraping a skin until it is very thin. Slunk vellum skins can be used to great effect, especially if you colour the reverse of the skin in some way.

Bookbinder's vellum

Vellum is also used by bookbinders, and their vellum is usually quite thick and tough. However, it also often has strong markings which are distinctive and very attractive. Use bookbinder's vellum, prepared only on the hairside, for pieces where you can use this distinctive colouring.

Kelmscott vellum

This was vellum especially prepared for William Morris and the books he printed on vellum at the Kelmscott Press. The skin is usually filled with chalk, which takes the printing ink well. This almost shiny, smooth, very white surface is also good for painting and illuminating, but not for calligraphy.

Parchment

Parchment is sheepskin which is normally split. It is quite thin and sometimes transparent. It is also greasy, and not the surface which any calligrapher would choose to use. In addition mistakes cannot be erased on parchment without their being obvious – a major drawback!

Goatskin

Goatskin can be used for calligraphy although its rather bumpy surface is not ideal. It is available as white and natural – which is more coloured.

Dealing with skins

If you have the choice, it is more economical to buy a whole skin. This will be big enough for one very large piece or two smaller pieces. The off-cuts around the side will often be wide enough for small manuscript painting or decorated initials, and any tiny postage-stamp size pieces remaining can be used for small gilded and decorated initial letters or monograms to give to friends. Finally the snippets and scraps left can be used for vellum size, see page 72.

A whole skin is expensive, however, and at first you may prefer to buy pieces cut to size.

It depends how long it has been in store as to how much preparation a piece of vellum will need, but I always presume that the grease needs to be removed. This is necessary for both painting and writing on a skin. Grease is best removed by using pounce powder; see page 89 for this.

The areas where there is to be writing should also have the nap of the skin raised. In mediæval times this was done by scraping with a knife. Nowadays, this is more effectively done by rubbing over these areas with fine grade sandpaper, or wet and dry. I used to use 300 grade followed by 600. Recently I have used just the coarser 300 or 400 grade and found the surface to be perfectly acceptable for calligraphy. Raising the nap means that the pen nib does not skate over the surface; it has a 'tooth'. However, before writing, brush the dust from the sandpaper away and rub over the area with powdered gum sandarac, see page 76. This acts as a resist and very slightly shrinks the lettering, thus achieving the very fine hair lines and serifs which you can see on early manuscripts.

Framing vellum

Although a specialist framer is preferred – one who knows how to handle and store vellum – framing pieces on vellum should not be too difficult if you explain the problems carefully to a framer.

The vellum, as a skin, is always trying to get back to animal shape, and moves as the atmosphere changes. Damp and heat will make the vellum cockle. (If it is stretched, vellum does not cause these problems. For stretching vellum, consult a specialist book such as ***Teach Yourself Calligraphy***.) The vellum should be attached to a mount or frame along one edge only. In addition there should be a 'slip' or small piece of frame between the glass and the vellum. This prevents the vellum from touching the glass. If it does so, some of the gold or paint may come off on to the underneath surface of the glass.

Other surfaces

There are many different surfaces which can be used for calligraphy. Papyrus is an historic writing surface, made from layers of stripped papyrus reed which have been beaten together to form a single sheet. You can buy papyrus from specialist suppliers. It is not so easy to write on papyrus with a metal nib. Choose a very flexible quill or a one-stroke or pointed brush. Mistakes can be removed by scraping with a sharp knife.

Fabric is also a suitable medium for lettering, although here again a brush rather than a pen is best. You can letter with a one-stroke brush and gouache on finely woven material, such as sheeting, but if you want your lettering to withstand being washed, use one of the fabric paints which you can buy from most art and craft shops. Why not try very large lettering with a wallpaper brush or home decorating brush on a large piece of sheeting? You could also write a suitable calligraphic saying on fabric for curtains, a blind, cushions or a garden chair.

Inks

There are many calligraphy and other pen inks for sale, but not all of them are ideal for pen lettering. Some are very sticky, others watery, some produce a rather shiny finish, but relatively few give a really dense black letter which is what most calligraphers want.

Bottled inks

Waterproof inks contain shellac; this is what makes them waterproof. Shellac clogs the nib and makes writing very difficult. It is always best to avoid any ink which has the word *waterproof* on its labelling.

Inks produced for fountain pens are specially manufactured to pass through the feeding mechanism and the rather rigid nib. These inks are watery because of this, and although perfectly satisfactory for practice they will show where you have gone over a stroke, or your pencil guidelines, on a best piece. The colour range is also rather limited. Unless you want a piece with watery writing, which you can achieve in other ways by using dilute gouache or watercolour, then reserve fountain pen inks for fountain pens.

Some of the inks produced for calligraphy are beautiful, dense inks which feed well through a dip pen. Others are very sticky and some slimy. It is best to ask friends and colleagues what ink they prefer before you buy, although perhaps it should be pointed out that manufacturers do change the make-up of inks and, as well as this, ink which someone else uses may not be to your taste. All is not lost if the ink you buy is rather thick and sticky, simply add drops of water to it until it is the consistency you prefer.

Stick inks

Most Chinese and Japanese stick inks are suitable for calligraphers. Sticks of black, red and other coloured inks are made into solid sticks which must then be ground on a ground glass slab or a special inkstone with water to reconstitute them as coloured liquids.

There are differences between Japanese and Chinese inks, and between inks made from other countries such as Korea. However, as Japanese and Chinese are most frequently available outside of those countries I shall focus on those.

The inks are made from a variety of smokes which are collected and combined with glue. The quality of the material from which the smoke is collected determines that of the ink. Most Chinese ink sticks should be allowed to mature and not used straight away.

The smoke for inks is collected from three different sources. The finest quality is the smoke from vegetable oil – rapeseed, sesame and paulownia oil. The size of the wick affects the quality of the smoke, as a thinner wick will produce smaller soot particles which produce a finer ink, often a blue-black in colour. The soot particles are collected on a concave dish or funnel and the ink does not change much with age as it contains so few impurities.

Ink made from pine smoke is the next finest ink, and the smoke is usually collected on paper. The soot particles are larger and there are more impurities with this ink.

Lastly, ink can be made from a variety of 'synthetic' sources such as gas and creosote. Here the quality differs according to the source material. Most of the stick inks available in European shops are from this synthetic source.

Japanese stick ink

The finer Japanese stick inks are sold wrapped in paper in wooden boxes. There are different sizes of ink ranging from 15g to 150g. Japanese ink is usually very densely black, but it can be less permanent than Chinese and may become granular after a few years. Japanese ink does not need to mature for as long a time as Chinese, in fact it is better to use it when it is still young.

Chinese stick ink

Chinese inks are sold in different sizes and sometimes in different forms. Ink is one of the four treasures of the craft, the others being the ink stone, paper and the brush. Ink is highly valued in China, and decorated sticks are often given as gifts. Sometimes the ink is made into various shapes such as turtles, fish and figures. This is ink more for show than to use.

Chinese ink needs time to mature, sometimes as long as 10 years, and many scribes use inks which are thirty or forty years old. This ink is more permanent than Japanese stick inks.

Choosing stick inks

Labelling on the inks available to calligraphers outside China and Japan can be a little confusing. Two inks may have what seem identical markings but be different colours! Paying more for one ink stick does not necessarily mean that it is better, either.

The information that you need for Chinese stick inks is usually at the end of each stick. These are the characters you should note:

油煙墨　　松煙墨

合成油煙墨

Top left: Vegetable oil smoke, Top right: Pine smoke, Below: Synthetic oil smoke

Making liquid ink from ink sticks

You will need a ground glass slab or a special ink stone for grinding the ink. Plain ink stones are not expensive and a smooth, functional slate or similar stone will grind your ink stick satisfactorily. However, some ink stones, similar to ink sticks, are made more for decoration than use. Here they may be carved with trees, foliage and rocks. Chinese scribes treasure their ink stones, which may have an uplifting text in Chinese characters around the side.

Rectangular ink stones have a slight depression at one end for collecting the ink. Square or circular ink stones may have a groove for pouring the ink into another container.

Pour some water, preferably distilled, into the well of the ink stone, if there is one. You will need about 3 – 5ml or between half and one teaspoonful. Place the stick ink in the water, and use the whole area of the stone to grind the ink. You will need to grind in a steady way, but make sure that it is grinding and not just stirring. Gradually the water will darken with the colour of the ink. When it

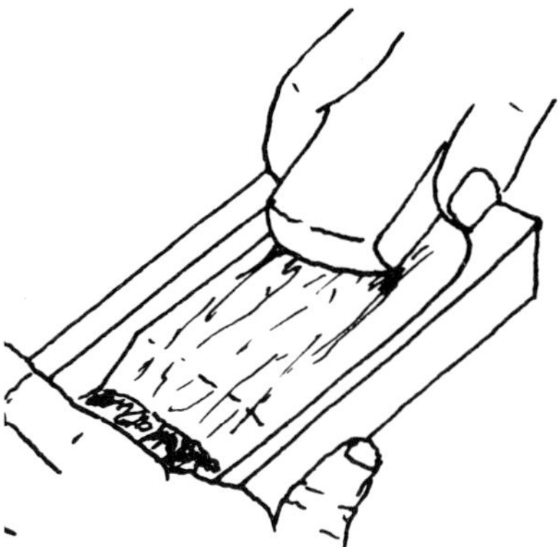

Pour some water into the well in the ink stone and grind the ink stick.

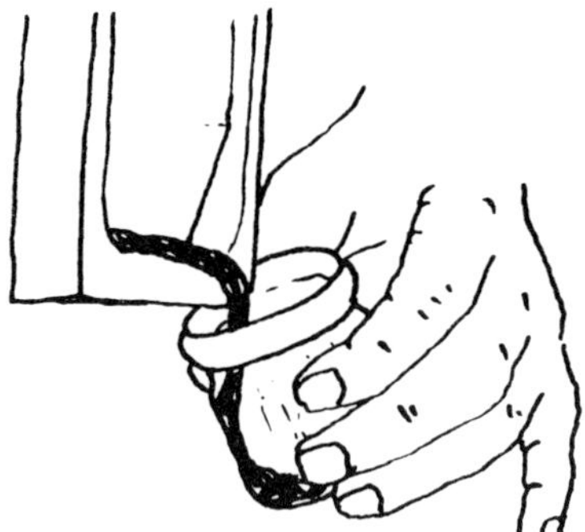

Decant the ink into a container if necessary.

is the consistency of thin cream, try the liquid in a pen. It should make a dense stroke on paper. Grind more to make the colour stronger, or add water to dilute accordingly.

Stick ink does not last for more than about a week once it has been ground, so it is a false economy to grind the whole stick.

To repeat the density exactly, count out a number of drops of water and grind for a set length of time each time you grind the ink. There is no set number of drops or seconds for this as stick inks vary a great deal.

Making your own ink

You can make your own ink from oak galls, which are the hard, round brown nodules, a little like marbles, on oak trees. They are the result of a gall wasp laying its egg on an oak twig and should not be confused with oak apples. The oak galls are hard and you may sometimes see a little hole where the gall wasp has emerged.

To make your own ink collect 80gm of oak galls. Wrap them in layers of newspaper and smash them into chunks with a hammer on a hard surface outside. Place the chunks in a glass jam jar.

Now cover the crushed galls with rainwater and leave to sit in the sun – perhaps on a sunny window sill – for a couple of days.

The resulting pale brown solution is changed into black by adding copperas or ferrous sulphate. Crush 50gm ferrous sulphate and stir it into the liquid. Stir and leave for another two days. Grind up 25gm of gum arabic (see page 75) and add this to the black liquid. The gum arabic will make the ink adhere to the paper or vellum and also thicken the mix. Allow it to stand for another day in the sun and then strain through muslin or a fine mesh nylon tea strainer.

The ink should be strained again when a sediment forms. Its strength of hue increases with exposure to the air.

Paints

To write good letters calligraphers need a liquid which is the consistency of thin, runny cream, thicker than that which would pass through a fountain pen. Most manufactured inks are too watery for calligraphy, unless they are specially made for the purpose; even then some of these can even be a little sticky and thick. For these reasons, scribes often use paint, which they can mix themselves, as ink.

Watercolour is used by many artists; it gives a transparent wash on paper. Gouache, pronounced goo-arsh, is similar to watercolour paints but it has a chalk or blanc fixe (artificial barium sulphate) base which makes it opaque. Tubes of gouache are slightly larger than those of watercolour because of this. Both watercolour and gouache can be used for lettering, but watercolour, by its very nature, will show through what is underneath, particularly any guidelines which may have been drawn, so calligraphers usually prefer gouache.

Gouache is suitable for both painting and lettering. It provides a dense consistent colour which mostly works well with a pen when diluted to the correct consistency. Gouache is the closest manufactured paint to egg tempera which was used extensively in mediæval manuscripts.

It is best to try out tubes of different manufacturers' gouaches to ensure that they are suitable for calligraphy, but this is rarely feasible. Do ask friends and colleagues which colours and products they find work well. As a general rule the better the quality of gouache the more finely it is ground and the better it works with a pen. For this reason choose Artists' colours rather than Designers'.

In addition, Designers' colours are most often used in artwork for reproduction, work which is not expected to last very long. Colours in this series are not particularly fast, and often quite fugitive. Buy Artists' quality paints and also check the permanence rating, which is usually shown by a letter, number or a line of stars on the tube itself. Reds in particular are very fugitive.

Although all colours of gouache are suitable for painting, not all work well with a pen as some can be rather greasy and not cover well and others separate out into grains; others can be rather gritty. It is important to have a consistent flow through the pen when using paints as ink.

The Colours

Originally the colours used for paints were made from particular animals, vegetables and minerals. Plants, such as woad *(Isatis tinctoria)* and indigo *(Indigofera tinctoria)* both produce blues. Animal products provide a range of colours, such as ivory which, when burnt, makes ivory black; sepia, from the ink sac of the cuttle fish or squid is a dark brownish black. The mollusc *Murex Brandaris* yields a beautiful purple dye; each animal provides just one drop of a white liquid, which used to be squeezed by hand from a little vein or cyst. When this is exposed to sunlight it produces a deep crimson purple – the colour of the togas of Roman emperors and also that of dyed vellum in early manuscript books. Whelks found round the shores of the British Isles also give a similar purple dye used in early English, French and Irish manuscripts. Minerals produce the blue of ultramarine from the semi-precious stone lapis lazuli, and there are also the earth colours of the Siennas and ochres.

Making or manufacturing paints from other than pure animal, vegetable or ground mineral sources has a very long history. Egyptian blue was made from copper calcium silicate before 2,000BC; verdigris and red and yellow oxides of lead were used in classical times. Prussian blue was the first truly artificial or synthetic colour produced, in Germany in 1704, and since then many of the rarer or more difficult to obtain colours have been replaced by manufactured pigments.

As the users of paints we have benefited greatly from this. In mediæval times pigments had to be ground, mixed with gum or egg yolk in the correct proportions and then diluted with water before they could be used. It usually fell to the apprentice to mix up the paints, a more technically difficult job than it would seem at first. Orpiment, for example, a rich lemon yellow when pure, was coarsely ground otherwise it lost its glorious colour, so, too, was azurite, where fine grinding resulted in a pale and weak blue instead of the deep almost violet-blue. Other pigments respond well to fine grinding, and would have been a joy to work with, compared with the rather gritty texture of some of the colours. Those made from vegetable matter, which was often boiled or soaked to remove the dye, would evaporate down to a fine powder. The problem with some of these, however, was getting them to mix with water because they were so fine. Being an apprentice to a mediæval scribe was no easy job!

Selecting Paints

Various gums and fillers are added to powdered pigment to make it adhere to the paper, to keep it pliable in the tube, to preserve it and to make it opaque. These are fully mixed into the paint and help to keep the paint usable for two or three years at least.

When selecting a tube of gouache it should be from fresh stock so that it will last as long as possible. The paint in the tube should be soft and pliable.

Choose the best quality of gouache that you can afford as it should then be better ground, therefore smoother and thus pass through the pen nib more easily.

Colours of gouache can be mixed in the same way as any other paints, so it is not necessary to buy up a vast range of colours. It is not a good idea to mix more than three colours together, though, so start with a few basic colours and build your purchase of tubes on those.

The exact colour of these named paints may vary with different makes, so do check the colour before you buy a particular shade you want. Manufacturers mix together different pigments to produce paints of the same name. It is probably not a good idea, either, to mix paints from different manufacturers.

Choosing a palette of colours

Although gouache colours can be mixed it does take time to match colours exactly or to repeat exactly an already mixed colour, and you may prefer to have more than just a couple of reds, blues and yellows. As well as this, certain colours have a texture not very suited to being used in a calligraphy dip pen. Calligraphers should look out for finely ground pigments which work well with a broad edge nib pen and also ones which have good coverage or hiding power, so that guidelines are covered by the paint from the letters. When used in miniature painting, the use of egg yolk as the binding medium usually adds opacity.

This list may save you wasted effort and money, although it should be emphasised that paints from the different manufacturers may well be different in texture and coverage, even though the colour name appears to be the same.

This list is not comprehensive but does cover most of the common pigments which you may need as a calligrapher and miniaturist.

Blacks

CARBON BLACK a deep intense brownish-black produced by burning organic matter such as oil and wood. It can be quite grainy, although it mixes well with water; however it does not write particularly well.

IVORY BLACK originally this paint was made from burning ivory waste and was a fine, intense black. Nowadays it is more usually made from bone. It is a dense black, sometimes slightly brownish and is quite smooth.

JET BLACK, VELVET BLACK this is a very smooth intensely black paint, which mixes well with water and is an excellent substitute for Chinese ink. It works very well with both broad-edge nibs and Copperplate pens.

LAMP BLACK this is nearly pure carbon, is slightly blue in colour and makes good neutral greys. It does not mix particularly well with water as it is a little fluffy and can seem almost greasy.

Whites

Bleedproof White this dense white gives great coverage, and, as its name suggests, does not bleed into other paints or areas, although it can be mixed with other colours. It can be rather thick even when diluted with water, and may seem a little greasy when used with a pen.

Lead White, Flake White lead white is highly poisonous because of its lead content. Its properties for calligraphers do not make it particularly valuable, and because it needs to be handled carefully it is probably best avoided.

Permanent White is not available in all ranges but is a dense white made from blanc fixe, or artificial barium sulphate. The paint can be used on its own or mixed with other paints. It works well through a calligraphy pen.

Zinc white, Chinese white this has now replaced lead white to a great extent. Although it is usually recommended as a mixing white it has a tendency to separate out from the mix and float on the surface of the palette as the particles are very fine indeed. This problem, and the fact that it does not have particularly good coverage as it is rather transparent, means that other whites may be better – given the choice.

Titanium White, Titan White this is a very pure white and has great coverage. It is a good white to use both for mixing and on its own. If buying only one white then this white or permanent white are good whites to choose.

Reds

Alizarin Crimson, Madder Lake this derived originally from the madder root. Alizarin was the first of the natural dyes to be made synthetically. It can be rather transparent although it is quite lightfast. Alizarin is an interesting colour – a rich, dark cool red – and it mixes well with other colours.

Cadmium Red this is a deep bright red which has now almost replaced vermilion. Most makes of cadmium red are smooth and work well with a pen.

CARMINE RED, CRIMSON LAKE is made from the dried bodies of the female insect *Coccus Cacti*, known also as cochineal. It is a scarlet red which is not very permanent to light as it turns brown eventually. Other colours are preferable.

ENGLISH RED, IRON OXIDE RED or RED OCHRE, INDIAN RED, VENETIAN RED, TUSCAN RED, MARS RED all are variations on a warm or dark red, which can extend to almost purple or maroon. The gouache is usually finely ground and the colours cover well.

My preference is for red ochre which has a history going back to classical times. A very dilute solution of red ochre is ideal for outlining an illustration which has been transferred to vellum or paper. This colour mixes well with white and makes a good shade of pink.

LEAD RED, MINIUM is a bright orangey-red with good coverage and a very fine texture. It was used in manuscript paintings for centuries; the word miniature derives from minium. It does turn brown however when exposed to light.

SCARLET VERMILION is close to the colour of vermilion used in mediæval times, but is perhaps a little pink. It needs to be mixed with orange to bring up the colour to a truer vermilion. The paint is finely ground and works well with a pen.

VERMILION, ENGLISH VERMILION, CHINESE VERMILION is red mercuric sulphide which is found also in cinnabar. It was originally also called minium, a name which was later given to red lead. Vermilion was used by the Chinese as red ink for writing and also for seals or chops on documents.

Real vermilion was expensive in early times and still is now. It is not easy to find tubes of real vermilion gouache but it is available as a powdered pigment. Vermilion covers well, but is affected by direct light. The fact that so many mediæval miniatures still have their jewel-like colours is because they were kept well away from daylight within the covers of books. As there are good substitutes for vermilion it is not really worth using this colour in calligraphy. However it is available as stick ink and here it is a good idea to take the trouble to prepare it for pen work. (See stick inks, page 30)

Blues

CERULEAN BLUE this is a stable colour which is rarely affected by light. It is slightly greeny-blue, a cool blue, and is a valuable pigment to have in the palette. However, it can be a little greasy and it is often best to mix with a little white or other colour to reduce this.

COBALT BLUE is not affected by sunlight and is an almost pure blue. It is one of the more expensive blues, but well worth having. The paint can be a little grainy for calligraphers, and again a tiny amount of another colour does help to alleviate this.

EGYPTIAN BLUE, BLUE FRIT, POMPEIAN BLUE is quite difficult to obtain nowadays, but is a colour with a great history. It is the blue of classical times, and was used as early as the Fourth Dynasty in Egypt (2613 – 2494BC). The exact method of making Egyptian blue was lost during the third to eighth centuries, but Pompeian blue has now replaced the colour, and is in fact purer and more finely ground.

INDIGO woad was used more often in northern Europe, and originally the use of indigo in northern Europe was controlled by law, where it was said to be 'a devilish drug and injurious to fabrics'! However, it is a good colour for calligraphers although it is rather fugitive. It is a dark almost violet-blue, and works very well in a pen. Although it can be rather dominant, red ochre and indigo used together on a piece of work is a striking combination which is one of my favourites.

MANGANESE BLUE is a much newer blue than others in this list, introduced only in 1935. It can be rather course and grainy and there are other slightly greeny-blue pigments which would be preferred.

PHTHALOCYANINE BLUE (THALO), MONASTRAL BLUE, WINSOR BLUE and other names, some rather exotic. This is a very vibrant deep greenish-blue which can be a little overpowering. It is usually smoothly ground.

PRUSSIAN BLUE, BERLIN BLUE, PARIS BLUE, ANTWERP BLUE, CHINESE BLUE this is a deep blue, slightly tinged with green. It has a very high tinting strength and only tiny amounts will need to be added to other colours in a mix. It is usually smoothly ground, although some makes can be a little greasy.

ULTRAMARINE, FRENCH ULTRAMARINE, PERMANENT BLUE originally produced from the semi-precious mineral lapis lazuli, ultramarine is a hot blue which is well worth having in your initial collection not least because of its ability to be mixed with other colours to produce pure hues. It is usually well ground, and although I find the colour unmixed a little bland, is a good consistency of paint to use for calligraphy.

Yellows

AUREOLIN, COBALT YELLOW one of the pure yellows with a reasonable covering power. Its expense is a detraction, however.

BRILLIANT YELLOW, PERMANENT YELLOW DEEP are both bright, slightly orange yellow, which are well ground and work well with a calligraphy dip pen.

CADMIUM YELLOW, CADMIUM YELLOW LITHOPONE this is a warm yellow which sometimes has a very slight orange tinge. It is a good colour to have in a first palette because it mixes well with other colours to produce a range of other pure colours. It is a finely ground paint which works well with the pen.

CHROME YELLOW is an important colour of the commercially made yellows but the colour will fade or become brown in time. Other yellows, such as cadmium yellow, are probably a better buy because they are more permanent.

GAMBOGE yellow gum resin from the tree of the genus *Garcinia* produced this colour. It is not very permanent and fades quickly in sunlight, although between the covers of a book, gamboge in manuscript paintings has survived the centuries. Mixed with Prussian blue it makes Hooker's green.

INDIAN YELLOW originally this was an extract prepared in India from the urine of cows which were fed on mango leaves. Perhaps it is reassuring to know that Indian yellow is now produced synthetically! It is a rich deep yellow, almost orange in colour, and very finely ground. It is a good colour for the calligrapher to have.

LEMON YELLOW, BARIUM YELLOW is a very stable colour which has a slight tinge of green. Lemon yellow can be a little transparent and does not cover well. However, it is a good colour to have as a mixing yellow.

NAPLES YELLOW, ANTIMONY YELLOW, JAUNE BRILLIANT was originally made from lead antimoniate, but is now more usually a mix of cadmium yellow, white and a little red. It is an unusual, dull yellow, which I find rather attractive. For the calligrapher it is a dream colour, as it is so finely ground and has good coverage.

Greens

CINNABAR GREEN, CHROME GREEN, MOSS GREEN, OLIVE GREEN these are simply mixes of Prussian blue and chrome yellow, combinations of which you may choose to do yourself. The manufactured variety of paints have good covering power and are usually finely ground.

COBALT GREEN, RINMANN'S GREEN, ZINC GREEN is a green with a slightly bluish tinge, which does not have great covering power. It is also usually very expensive and only really for the purist.

EMERALD GREEN, SCHWEINFURT GREEN, PARIS GREEN, PERMANENT GREEN LIGHT (sometimes) can be a rather gritty colour, which some find insipid. This bright blue-green is not really worth a place in a first palette, nor, in my opinion, in a second!

HOOKER'S GREEN a mixture of Prussian blue and gamboge. This is an interesting colour, but it is probably better to mix your own rather than buy a tube of paint which you may not use very often. It is a deep bluey-green.

OXIDE OF CHROMIUM, VIRIDIAN MATTE this is one of the best paints for calligraphers. It is so smoothly ground that it reacts as an ink, covers very well, and is also very permanent. It is a pity that the colour is so dull! I like to mix a little indigo to spice it up a little. Try it on its own and then add whatever colour you think best for the piece you are working on.

PERMANENT GREEN is a mixture of viridian with cadmium or zinc yellow. It is smoothly ground, but perhaps rather a dull middle green for much use, and is easier to mix your own.

PHTHALOCYANINE GREEN (THALO) this is similar to viridian but it is more intense. It is a permanent green which is finely ground.

SAP GREEN can be rather a dull green in hue, and the paints sold under this name are not consistent from manufacturer to manufacturer. It is better to mix your own with ultramarine and cadmium yellow. Originally it was made from the ripened berries of the blackthorn, *Rhamnus.*

TERRE VERTE, GREEN EARTH this is a naturally occurring pigment, which ranges from a yellow-green to a pale greenish-gray. In tubes it is usually a neutral sage green, which has a low covering capacity. It is an unusual colour, but does have its attractions for the calligrapher.

VIRIDIAN, GUIGNET'S GREEN this is a cool, pure green, but can be rather grainy for use in calligraphy, which is a pity because the colour is beautiful.

Violets

ALIZARIN VIOLET this is not really very permanent and although well ground and a clear purple lake, it is better to choose another paint.

COBALT VIOLET DARK and LIGHT the dark or deep is a blue-violet and the light a reddish purple. Both are well ground and suitable for calligraphy.

LIGHT PURPLE a mid purple which mixes well with other colours and gives good coverage.

LIGHTPROOF VIOLET, SPECTRUM VIOLET well ground violet colours, more blue than red.

MAGENTA this is a rich red purple colour which is very smoothly ground as a gouache and a joy for the calligrapher to use, unfortunately it is not very permanent.

MANGANESE VIOLET, PERMANENT VIOLET this is a good violet colour, but it can be a little insipid. It works well with the pen as it is finely ground.

ULTRAMARINE VIOLET a blue violet which is finely ground and good with a calligraphy pen.

Oranges

CADMIUM ORANGE this is manufactured from cadmium sulphide which is used to make cadmium yellow. It can be a deep orange which has a good covering power and is well ground.

ORANGE LAKE LIGHT this colour can be mixed with scarlet vermilion to give a better orange-red for manuscript work. It is finely ground but a little startling on its own!

Browns

BURNT SIENNA From Sienna in Tuscany, raw Sienna is burnt or roasted and so changes to a warm, reddish brown. Burnt Sienna is a good colour to have because of its mixing qualities. Mixed with ultramarine it forms a good warm grey.

BURNT UMBER is made by roasting raw umber until it changes to a warm red brown. Burnt umber can be a little sticky and granular, but it is preferred to Vandyke brown which it resembles.

CAPUT MORTUUM this is a bluish red iron oxide which is an interesting colour to use for calligraphy.

RAW SIENNA is a yellow ochre which gets its name from Sienna in Tuscany. It is warmer, more orange than raw umber, and can sometimes be a little sticky.

RAW UMBER the umbers are similar to the ochres and Siennas but they contain manganese dioxide as well as the iron oxide. The colour is a warm yellow-brown with a tinge of green. It works well with a pen.

SEPIA used to be produced from the ink sac of the cuttlefish, but is now a mixture of burnt Sienna and lampblack. Perhaps it is better to mix your own. It works well with the pen.

VANDYKE BROWN is a sticky dark brown pigment which is produced from brown coal or lignite. It hardens quite quickly in the tube, and can be a little grainy. It is not the world's most exciting colour.

YELLOW OCHRE, MARS YELLOW has been used as a pigment since classical times, and even before then. Yellow ochre is a yellow with a tinge of brown and is permanent. It is finely ground and has good coverage.

Greys

MIXING GREYS, NEUTRAL GREYS these are manufactured greys which can be used on their own or added to other colours. They are generally rather dull, and it would be much better to mix your own.

NEUTRAL TINT is a watercolour made from a mixture of India ink, phthalocyanine blue and a little alizarin. It has limited uses for calligraphy.

PAYNE'S GREY this is a soft opaque blue-grey which is most attractive. It does not cover well, however, and you may prefer to mix your own with ultramarine, a little black and red ochre to soften the colour.

The first group of colours for a new calligrapher

It is very difficult when starting out on a new enthusiasm such as calligraphy to be faced with the whole variety of new tools and materials which may be needed. It is even more difficult to be in an art shop and be faced with a whole range of paint tubes of every hue, and be at a loss to know what to buy first.

Before you part with any money, do check through the first part of this chapter. Make sure that the permanence is what you want, and that you are not paying more for expensive colours which are not so useful to calligraphers.

You can mix colours from a minimum range, and as a very first purchase and for calligraphy I would suggest the following:

Jet or Velvet Black
Titanium white
Cadmium Red – red tending towards *orange*
Alizarin Crimson – red tending towards *violet*
Ultramarine – blue tending towards *violet*

Cerulean Blue – blue tending towards *green*
Lemon Yellow – yellow tending towards *green*
Cadmium Yellow – yellow tending towards *orange*

(Apart from the black and white these are the basic colours recommended by Michael Wilcox in his book Blue and Yellow Don't Make Green[1] *which is recommended reading if you are unsure about colours and their mixing).*

The limited range of colours here consist of pairs of primary colours. For best results to make a clear mix of a secondary colour use only those colours which are linked by a tendency towards that secondary colour.

From these you can mix almost any combination:

For a clear ***violet*** mix **alizarin crimson** and **ultramarine**
For a clear ***green*** mix **lemon yellow** and **cerulean**
For a clear ***orange*** mix **cadmium yellow** and **cadmium red**

Different **greys** and **browns** can be made from mixing:
either of the **yellows,** with **alizarin** and **ultramarine**
either of the **blues** with **cadmium red** and **cadmium yellow**
either of the **reds** with **lemon yellow** and **cerulean**

Try experimenting with these colours until you find ones that you like. It is a good idea to keep a written record together with a small patch of the paint so that you can refer to it later.

And then...

It is likely that you will then want to extend your range of colours. Mixing colours is fun to do, but there many well be occasions when you want to repeat a colour, or simply want to write in a particular colour straight from the tube, mixed only with water. I have a group of colours, in addition to those listed above which I have used for many years, sometimes mixing them with others and sometimes on their own.

These are colours which I would recommend for calligraphy:

Red Ochre
Venetian Red

Scarlet Vermilion (mixed with Orange Lake Light)
Indigo
Prussian Blue
Naples Yellow
Oxide of Chromium
Terre Verte
Spectrum Violet/Ultramarine Violet
Purple Lake
Magenta
Orange Lake Light (mixed with Scarlet Vermilion)
Burnt Sienna
Caput Mortuum
Raw Sienna
Raw Umber

This list does veer towards the earth colours, and perhaps emphasises my work on manuscript painting.

Using paints

Start out with the tools and materials best suited for the purpose. For paints try to use a white palette, saucer or plate. The white background colour will show the paint at its truest hue. An old brown saucer will not give the same effect. At first perhaps it does not seem important to have an exact representation of a particular colour – 'near enough is good enough' – however, matching colours will be important later on.

When you remove the cap from a tube of paint there is often a sticky gum which is used by manufacturers to prevent air getting in the tube and affecting the paint. Squeeze the tube gently and wipe this gum away on a piece of paper kitchen towel or an old cloth.

Now squeeze out about 1cm or half an inch from the tube on to the palette. Add drops of water using an old brush, the cheapest brushes from a market stall are sufficient. Do not use your best brushes to mix paint, because the action will force paint high up into the hairs and this will be difficult to remove. You may, if you prefer, add water to the paint using an ink dropper.

Mix the water into the paint until it is the consistency of thin runny cream. Always mix up all the paint you have squeezed out into the palette. If you leave a lump of unmixed paint on the side it will gradually dissolve in the water and affect the consistency of the liquid you are using.

Test the colour on a piece of scrap paper, the same quality as that you are intending to use for a best piece. Make sure that the colour lies flat and smooth, and that it is not grainy, sticky, or too thin. Adjust the consistency, adding a little more paint if it is too thin and a little more water if it is too sticky.

Feed the ink into your calligraphy pen using the mixing brush. Stroke the brush on the side or near to the tip of the nib. If there is a blob of paint on top of the nib wipe this off on to a paper kitchen towel before you start writing. Again test the paint for its writing qualities before you start on your best paper.

You do not have to wash up the palette at the end of each writing session. Cover the paint loosely with another saucer or palette to keep the dust off. The water may well evaporate before you come to use it again, but you simply add water as before.

Your brushes and pen, however, should be washed carefully and dried before storage.

Problems with paints

Paints are manufactured for painting, not writing, and there may be some problems for calligraphers. If the paint is gritty or grainy, then the paint can be reground with a large glass muller (made for grinding pigments) on a ground glass slab, but it is probably better to choose another more suitable paint of similar hue.

If the paint is sticky or greasy you can improve the viscosity of it by adding a drop or two of ox gall. This is a colourless solution which lessens the surface tension and produces a better flow. Be warned, however, ox gall has a foul smell! Too much ox gall will make the paint difficult to handle.

Sometimes the paint does not seem to stick well to the paper, and comes off on to the opposite page, or can even be brushed off with the hand or an eraser. This can be remedied by adding gum arabic solution to the paint, again only a drop or two. This will make the paint stickier, so care is needed here when writing.

It is a good idea to add a drop or two of gum arabic if you have left the paint in a palette for a long time. Some of the adhering qualities may have evaporated with the water, and the gum arabic drops will replenish them. Always test the paint before you do this, and test again after you have added the gum.

Mixing paints

As a rule of thumb, always add dark colours to light rather than the other way round. Dark colours are dominant and you will need to add much more light colour to a dark pigment to have any effect than if you had added a little of the dark to the lighter colour.

It is better to mix up sufficient paint for the task in hand, but there will be occasions when you will run out. For this reason it is a good idea to have a notebook with a record of what paints were used for that mix and a painted swatch of the colour, so that re-matching is easier than trying to remember exactly what paints went into making that particular colour.

If you are more careful with your mixing, then to re-mix will not always be a crisis, and although this may seem a fiddle at first, if you get into the habit of always mixing your paints like this, then you will have far fewer problems with re-mixing colours.

Squeeze a very small amount of the main colour paint from the tube. With a palette knife, wooden or plastic cocktail stick or similar, slice straight down the paint close to the tube. Discard this paint; the purpose is to get a straight edge of paint. Now squeeze the tube again and measure out a length of paint along a plastic ruler, say 1cm. Slice down again with the knife and replace the cap on the tube. Carefully scoop up all the paint and place in the palette or saucer. Do the same with the second colour, although in this case the amount of paint will be less than 1cm. Repeat this for a third colour if used. Write down the amounts of paint measured along the ruler.

Add a few drops of water and mix the colours together using an old brush. If you need to add any more colour, again squeeze a small amount along the ruler and note how much extra you have used. When the mix is the colour you want, add more water so that it is the consistency for writing. Paint a small amount of the colour in your record book next to the measurements.

When you want to repeat this colour, refer back to your notes and simply measure out the paint in the same proportions.

Removing paint (and mistakes!)

Gouache is not always easy to remove from clothes, so it is best to wear something old when lettering, and to protect any precious surfaces. Always cover your paper with a guard sheet when writing, the guard sheet also protects your work from any dirt or grease on your hands.

To remove gouache from paper or vellum is time consuming but not difficult, and you have to decide what stage you are at as to whether you try to remove the mistake or start again.

One method is to take a small shallow scoop out of the paper using a very sharp knife or scalpel. This is not always easy for the beginner, and is difficult for the expert if using a thin paper. As well as this, some papers are only surface sized. By removing the top surface, when you write on it again the paint will feather out and bleed on the patch of unsized paper.

The method which I have used successfully, and which beginners have not found too difficult, is to use clean water, a clean fine paint brush, pieces of clean white paper kitchen towel and a typewriter eraser, preferably the white variety manufactured as a pencil, where the end can be sharpened to a point.

If possible, blot the mistake with the kitchen towel as soon as the mistake has been noticed, to remove any wet ink or paint. You may well discover the mistake only when you have finished, however, which is when the ink has dried.

Dip the brush into the clean water. Wipe it on the side of the jar and paint over the mistake carefully. Immediately blot with the kitchen towel to remove the coloured water which will be produced. Do a little at a time, and be patient. Gradually the ink or paint will dissolve in the water and come off on to the kitchen towel.

It is unlikely, however, that all the paint will come out. If it does you are very lucky! Eventually, no more colour will appear on the kitchen towel, and all the paint or ink which can be removed has been removed.

Allow the area to dry completely. This could take a couple of hours, half a day, or it could be overnight. Do not be tempted to go on to the next stage until the paper is completely dry, however, as the paper could tear.

When the paper is dry, slowly and carefully rub over the mistake with the typewriter eraser. Eventually all the colour will be removed, and usually the surface of the paper becomes roughened.

Place a piece of thin paper, such as photocopying paper over the erased area and rub over with a bookbinder's bone folder, a burnisher or a smooth pebble or stone. This presses the paper fibres back down to a smooth surface and the sheet of thin paper prevents the paper itself from being burnished or going shiny.

Now you can write over the area and correct your mistake.

[1]Wilcox, Michael, *Blue and Yellow Don't Make Green*

Egg Tempera

Early scribes and artists had the time consuming and sometimes difficult job of having to obtain, grind and then mix all of the pigments or inks they were to use. Admittedly they did usually have the tremendous advantage of a trainee or apprentice to do the boring and unpleasant tasks, which left them to concentrate on the lettering and painting itself.

Each pigment usually had to be treated in a slightly different way, some powders would be so fine and fluffy that grinding in with water to a smooth liquid was a real problem, others produced a very sticky mix, and others still would have been a joy to use.

The fact that powdered pigment mixed with egg is virtually permanent is shown by the vibrant colours which shine up at us from manuscript books. In addition to this, egg tempera can be overpainted, so tones, shading and highlights can be added as an overlay, and mistakes can also be painted over.

Nowadays, most of the powdered pigments we use are much purer and also better ground than those which were used in the Middle Ages. The powder is fine, but should still be ground with water and mixed carefully.

The individual colours are usually sold by weight. This can be a little confusing at first because some colours, such as certain compounds of lead, weigh quite heavily, and you will only have a small amount, and others are light and almost fluffy and you will have more than you know what to do with.

It is a good idea to transfer the powdered pigment from the temporary paper wrapping to a glass jar. The jar should be airtight, and labelled carefully with the name of the pigment and the date it was purchased.

How to make Egg Tempera

A few people do make egg tempera without grinding the powdered pigment with water first but this is not something I would recommend. Some pigments are very light and they do not mix well with the egg yolk and water. Grinding the pigments seems to release the true beauty of their colour, and as the pigment and water mix can be kept indefinitely, it seems sensible to do this with all your powdered pigments, and store what you need in this way.

Slab and muller

Cennini[2] recommends the hard stone porphyry (or failing that, granite) for both slab and muller. However, both are difficult to obtain and very expensive. Most tempera artists use ground glass.

You will need a large ground glass slab, at least 30cm by 20cm or 12 inches by 9 inches, and a ground glass muller which is about 8 – 10cm or 4 inches in diameter for this process. It is best to have a plastic spatula to scrape the coloured paste off the slab; the sort of pliable kitchen spatula which scrapes a mixing bowl really clean is the best. A metallic kitchen palette knife is not really a good substitute as it can damage the surface of the glass.

Having the ground glass set into a wooden surround is recommended as there is a degree of pressure on the glass. If the supporting surface is not completely flat and rigid, the glass may crack under the strain.

Look carefully at the mullers before you buy one. There should be no scratches on the surface. Take care that there are no air bubbles just under the surface, either. Both the slab and muller will need to be reground periodically if they get a lot of use. As more of the glass is removed from the muller small air bubbles will appear as holes in the surface. Pigment will collect in these holes and could discolour other pigments during the grinding process.

Before you use either slab or muller it is an idea to prepare both by using some medium fine emery powder. Tip some on to the slab, add a few drops of water until it is a thin paste and then grind all over with the muller. Move the muller slightly on to its sides so that they are rubbed by the emery paste, too.

Wash the slab and muller carefully to remove all traces of the emery powder so that the pigments are not contaminated.

Grinding the pigments

Take one or two 5ml spoons or small teaspoonfuls of one of the powdered pigments and tip on the clean, washed glass slab. It does not matter how much of the powder you use, grind more or less according to your preference. However, it is a good idea not to measure out large amounts otherwise there will be too much on the surface of the slab; some will spill over the edge and there may be parts of the colour which are insufficiently ground and mixed.

Grind powdered pigment with distilled water in a figure of eight motion.

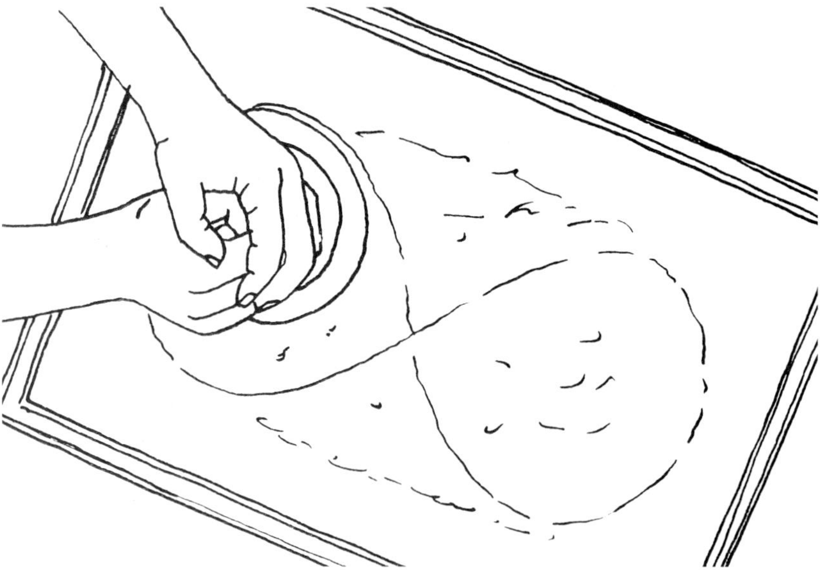

Some colours are permanent and staining so it is a good idea to wear old clothes or some form of protection for this, and also to protect the table surface with layers of old newspapers.

Add drops of distilled water to the powder pigment. You want to make the mixture into a paste, not so stiff that the muller does not move relatively easily over the slab, but not so wet that the paint runs over the edge of the slab. It does help to mix the powder with water first by using the plastic spatula.

Grind rhythmically and steadily with the muller, moving it in a figure of eight. You may find this process easier if you stand. If the muller becomes too sticky when moving over the slab then add more water. Gradually the pigment and water will mix together and become a smooth paste.

Using the flexible spatula, scrape the coloured paste from the slab and place it in a small glass jar with an airtight lid. When all the coloured paste has been removed from the slab fill the jar up to the top with distilled water, and check periodically that it is still covered by liquid. If the paste dries out then you will need to regrind it as before.

Label the jar with the colour of the pigment and the date it was ground. Store these jars upright away from bright sunlight.

Separating the egg

For making egg tempera it is best to try to get eggs as fresh as possible as the mixed paints will last longer than those mixed with stale eggs. In addition, eggs from chickens which are allowed to roam freely usually have a stronger yolk sac which makes removing the yolk from the sac easier.

It is only the yolk of the egg which is used for egg tempera painting and artists vary in their ways of preparing it. Some casually separate the yolk from the white, others strain the yolk from the sac through muslin, others are more meticulous in preparation.

I prefer to make sure that the yolk sac is as free from white as possible as too much egg white can make the paint rather stringy.

Place about three or four pieces of kitchen towel in a pile to one side of a surface. Tap the shell of an egg on the side of a cup or small basin to crack the shell and, holding it over that basin or cup, either use a manufactured egg separator or save the yolk in one half of the shell. Allow the white to fall into the cup and move the yolk from half egg shell to half egg shell so that as much of the white is removed as possible. Use the edges of the shell to cut through any stringy parts of the white.

When almost all of the white has fallen into the cup transfer the egg yolk to the palm of your hand. Wipe the other hand on the pile of kitchen towels. Slide the yolk into that hand and wipe the other hand on the kitchen towels. Repeat this until the yolk is as dry as possible. Moving the yolk sac from hand to hand in this way slightly cooks the sac and makes removing the yolk itself easier.

Have a clean cup, egg cup or white porcelain palette to hand and a sharp bladed knife, such as a scalpel or craft knife. If you are right handed, hold the yolk on the flat palm of your right hand and with your left hand pinch a little of the yolk sac and lift it up. (Left-handers should hold the yolk in their left hand.) Hold this over the cup or

Pinch the yolk sac and hold it between the finger and thumb of one hand and pierce it with a knife blade so that the yolk falls into a cup or white palette.

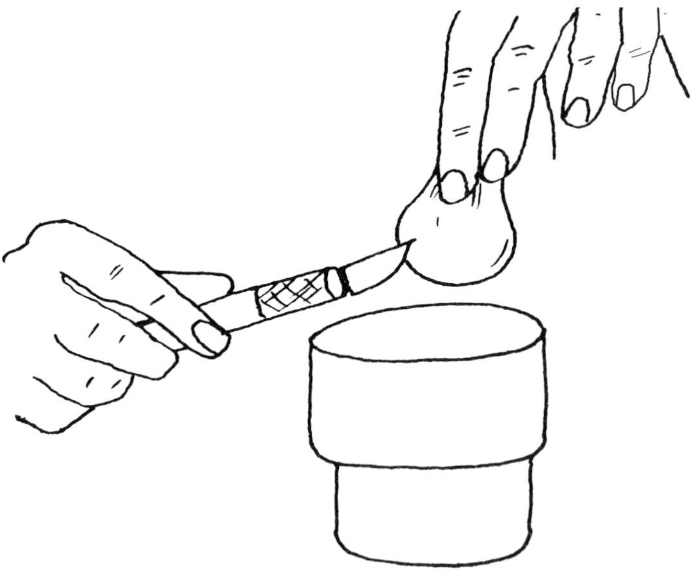

palette and with the knife pierce the sac so that all the yolk falls into it. You can press the sides of the egg sac together so that as much of the yolk as possible is squeezed out.

This gives a good pure yolk with very little white and which lasts for a few days. Some artists advocate adding a little vinegar or oil of cloves to the yolk to act as a preservative, but I feel that it is better to paint with the yolk when fresh, and simply to use another egg yolk when the first is stale.

Mixing the paint

The paint should contain sufficient yolk to make it adhere to the surface, but not so much that it is sticky and difficult to use. Too little yolk will make the paint chalky. The actual amounts for mixing depend on the individual pigments. Some require more yolk and others less. As well as this, some of the ground pigments separate out from their storage water and it is easy to scoop up some of the pigment, others are so fine that the they remain suspended completely in the water. Those which contain a lot of water while being stored will obviously require less water to mix than those which are more easily separated.

The generally accepted rule is to add equal amounts of egg yolk and water from the already ground colours, but because of the previous problems with the uneven quantities of powdered pigment and water, this is not always possible to judge easily.

Using egg tempera

Add water to the egg yolk and pigment mix until it is the consistency of thin, runny cream.

To test for correct consistency paint a small strip along a sheet of glass and allow it to dry. It should peel off with a knife in one strip without breaking.

If you want to mix two or more colours together, mix the different powder and water pastes first and then add the yolk when you are sure of your colour. In this way you can store mixes of colours in glass jars for use again. When it is mixed with egg yolk the paint has a limited life.

Painting with egg tempera

Egg tempera painting requires a controlled technique. The design must be fully worked out and only the outline transferred to paper or vellum before any paint touches the surface. It is a dry process, there are no large areas of washes as in watercolour painting.

Dip your brush into the paint, and then wipe the excess off on the edge of the palette or a clean paper kitchen towel before painting. There are two main ways of painting with tempera. Some artists prefer to outline the area first in a dilute mix of the colour, and then go over again with a stronger mix. Others prefer to fill in the areas of colour carefully and painstakingly with small strokes of a fine sable brush (see brushes, page 13). This painting process is similar to drawing with a pencil. Fill an area with body colour by a type of *wet in wet* method. Work out the best route around the area to be painted and then start in one corner. Gradually work your way around making sure that no edge ever dries out otherwise it will leave a line which will show.

Wash and dry your brushes frequently in water so that the yolk does not dry and harden in them.

Highlights and shadows can be painted over the egg tempera once it has dried, and this is one of the beauties of this method of painting. Other colours will sit quite happily on top of the surface paint.

At some point over the months the egg tempera dries to such a point where this cannot be done. Ralph Meyer[3] suggests that this is after about eight months.

During painting, place a dampened folded kitchen towel over the tops of your palettes to prevent them from drying out. Cover this loosely with plastic film and place in a refrigerator (not freezer) overnight. You will have about three to four days at the most to use this paint, so choose small paintings until you are certain of the method and become quicker.

[2] Cennini, d'Andrea Cennino, *Il Libro dell'Arte*

[3] Mayer, Ralph, *The Artist's Handbook of Materials and Techniques*,

Metallic Powders, Paints and Leaves

It is the brilliance of shiny gold, beaten into tissue-thin leaves, which combines so magnificently with lettering and miniature painting. The specific qualities of gold were well used by the illuminators – it did not tarnish, it could be beaten into the finest of leaves and it stuck to itself. Gold has remained untarnished and shining brightly in manuscript books for hundreds of years. However, powdered and leaf gold are both expensive and although they last for a very long time, this quality is not always one which is needed.

There are other metallic leaves and powders which are similar in colour to gold but which tarnish more quickly Their great advantage, though, is their cost, and with care they can be a good substitute for gold for more ephemeral pieces and for roughs and ideas. Silver substitute is often better than real silver because the latter tarnishes readily, within five years usually, and although the initial rainbow colouring may be attractive, it loses its effect when the painted area turns to black.

Metallic powders

Metallic powders are sold in two forms, that which already has some adhesive quality mixed in with the powder, and that which needs a glue or gum mixed to it to attach it to paper or vellum. If you buy real gold powder it will always need to be mixed with gum.

To try to determine which is which with metallic paints, if it is not obvious, mix a little of the powder with water and then either paint or write with the liquid. Allow it to dry. That which needs adhesive will be rubbed readily from the paper with your thumb. In addition, metallic powder which does not already have adhesive will often not mix readily with water, and will rarely form a liquid which can easily be used.

The powders already mixed with adhesive, which often use dry dextrin glue as the binder, need simply to be mixed with water to the required consistency and then used either through a brush or pen. (See page 62, Painting and writing with metallic liquids)

Bronze powders, which require a glue, range from a pale gold to the deepest bronze colour. They are usually mixed with an adhesive such as liquid gum arabic or Ormoline metallic paint medium to form a liquid which can be used as paint. The Ormoline mix may need some dilution with thinners before it can be used as ink, as the metallic particles are not particularly fine. Use brushes which are not best quality for mixing, and clean these immediately afterwards with thinners or liquid cleaner if using Ormoline. Then wash your brushes in warm soapy water otherwise they will harden and be unusable.

Bronze powders mixed with this medium can also be used to coat surfaces and build up textures. Crushed clean egg shells, sand and sugar amongst other things can all be coated with different colours of the bronzes to form interesting decorative contrast to your lettering.

Gold powder

Gold powder was sold for years by the pennyweight, and is now sold by the gramme. It needs to be mixed with gum arabic before it will stick to paper or vellum.

Tip 0·5g of gold powder into a tiny jam jar and add 10 drops of gum arabic and a little distilled water. Stir carefully; the result will look like mud! Fill the jar to the top with distilled water and stir again. Allow the gold to settle, this may take a few hours or even overnight. Carefully tip the excess water into another small jar and keep this for washing your brushes and pens – there may be some gold remaining in it.

Now try your gold paint on paper. When it is dry brush over it with your hand. If the paint comes off you will need to add a few more drops of gum arabic and repeat the process above. If it stays on the paper, place a piece of crystal parchment paper or glassine over it and rub over with a burnisher. Remove the paper and burnish directly. If there is not a good shine there is too much gum in the mix. Fill the jar to the top with distilled water again, stir, allow to settle and repeat the process.

It is a good idea to reserve a mixing and painting brush for gold only. This means that you can wash the brushes out in your little pot of distilled water to save any gold in them. If the brushes have been used for painting, the paint will contaminate the gold.

Metallic paints

A range of metallic powders already mixed with adhesive is available in the form of tubes and also pans of gold, silver, bronze and copper gouache.

Metallic gouache in pans or tubes

Metallic gouache is available in colours which range from silver, copper and bronze to pale and deep golds. All simply need to be mixed with water in a palette until they form a liquid which is the consistency of thin runny cream.

Gold paint or shell gold

Real gold is also sold in small rectangles of paint, about the size of a quarter pan of watercolour, with their own tiny circular white palettes. This is called *shell gold* because it used to be sold in mussel shells. The gold comes in a range of colours – jaune, rouge, citron, vert (yellow, red, lemon, green respectively). The slight and subtle change of colour is due to additional metals added to the gold which has already been mixed with gum arabic, and so needs simply to be diluted with water for use.

At first, you may have some trouble in using shell gold. The problem usually is not adding enough water. Add enough drops of distilled water to make a puddle in the gold, so that you have some liquid you can use. None of the gold will be wasted in so doing as what you do not use will dry in the palette, or be washed into the jar of distilled water to be used again.

When all the palette has been used, decant most of the water from the jar of washings. There will probably be enough gum arabic in the gold remaining to make it adhere to the paper or vellum. Try it. If not, add drops of gum arabic and prepare as you did for gold powder.

Shell gold can be burnished when it has dried and thus be made to shine, however, it will not shine as brightly as leaf gold. You can use a pencil burnisher to push patterns into shell gold, and it looks very effective if you paint a small diamond, burnish, and then twist the point of a pencil burnisher into the centre.

Painting and writing with metallic liquids

Metallic gouaches and real gold paints can be used for both painting and writing, and for both skills there is a technique for their use. Metallic and real gold paints consist of liquid and metallic particles, the latter being much larger than the pigment particles in non-metallic paints.

The metal will easily separate out from the liquid in the palette, and you will need to stir it with a brush frequently to keep the two mixed. This is especially true with gouache. Therefore stir every time you charge your pen or brush.

When using the paint these same metallic particles, being heavier than the liquid, will fall to the end of your pen or brush. After one, or at the most two strokes you will be writing or painting mainly with the medium. For this reason use small amounts of the paint in your pen and brush, and charge them frequently. I usually have the brush ready to stroke on the side of my pen after every letter, and often more frequently.

It often helps to make two or more thin coats of metallic paint over an area for painting, rather than trying to coat in one layer. The paint sits more happily in this way.

If you want to lay a watercolour or gouache wash and drop in metallic gouache, wait until the last moment before using the metal paint, otherwise it will sink to the bottom and not be seen. You may need to experiment with this.

Always clean your brushes and nibs carefully after using metallic paints, and wash your water pot thoroughly, too, otherwise you will find shiny particles in the next batch of paint you use, something which you may not want.

Burnishing metallic paints

When the paint is completely dry lay a piece of crystal parchment or glassine on top and rub over with a burnisher or polished stone. This will flatten the paint and it will then reflect the light better.

Some metallic gouaches can be burnished directly with a smooth and polished stone, although they will not shine as well as real gold paint, which in turn will not shine as well as gold leaf.

Because the particles are usually larger than gold, and may be harsher, it is probably better to reserve a burnisher specifically for polishing metallic paints. A cheaper alternative is to use a polished stone which you can buy from jewellery suppliers and even car boot sales! Rub over the paint directly with a burnisher or polished stone. You may be able to produce a reasonable shine. You can also push patterns into the softer metal paints with a pencil burnisher.

Metal leaves – Dutch metal or schlag, bookbinder's gold

Metal leaves, made from a mixture of zinc and copper, are available in both silver and gold colours and are sold in books of 25 leaves. The leaves are 14cm square and are not attached to the backing sheet – *loose* – or pressed hard and so stuck temporarily to the backing sheet – *transfer.* They are relatively cheap, but the leaves do not stick to themselves as real gold does. The silver Dutch metal has an advantage in that it does not tarnish, unlike real silver.

Bookbinder's and other metallic films are often sold in strips or in rolls. Some metallic films have laser patterns on them which, if a little gaudy, do make for lively contrast!

Using Dutch metal and other leaves

Metal leaves must be attached to paper or vellum with an adhesive. They do not stick readily to gesso, and as the leaves are cheap, it is not worth all the preparation that gesso requires. Use modern glues and adhesives, such as PVA, cryla or acrylic gloss medium, water gold size, gum ammoniac and so on (see pages 76 – 79).

Feed the adhesive into a pen or lay with a brush and allow to dry. Either cut off a piece of metallic film from the roll or hold the book of metal leaves by the sewn spine, fold the back cover so that it is away from the leaves and allow the loose leaves and backing sheets to fall on a clean surface. Carefully hold all the leaves and backing sheets together apart from the last one. Using a pair of clean scissors cut a piece of the metal leaf with its backing sheet. Put the rest of the book to one side where it will not be knocked. Now reactivate the stickiness in the gum you have used by breathing long and hard. Immediately place the piece of cut metal over the sticky area and press down firmly down with your fingers. Rub over the back, through the backing sheet, with a polished stone or burnisher. Some metals on certain glues can then be burnished directly. See pages 70 – 79 for this.

Gold, silver, platinum and palladium leaves

These precious metals are sold in books of 25 leaves which are 8cm square. They may be attached to the backing sheet – *transfer,* or unattached – *loose.* Confusingly in the USA, gold which is not attached to the backing sheet is called transfer gold, and that which is attached is called patent gold.

Gold for illuminating should be of high quality, at least 22·5 carat, and preferably 23 carat or more. It is a bright, shiny yellow. Silver and white gold (which has a high silver content) are also sold in books of 25 leaves but both tarnish quite quickly. The edges may become rainbow coloured and then turn black. Platinum is an expensive substitute for silver and is a slightly pinky-brown silver colour. Palladium is also expensive and is a more metallic, bluish silver colour.

There are also two main thicknesses of gold. Thin leaves of gold are called *single gold*, and thicker leaves *double* or *extra thick* gold. For burnishing most illuminators use single leaves followed by double leaves. If you have not gilded before then it is probably best to use single transfer followed by double loose. You will get a better burnish using loose leaves, but as this gold is difficult to handle it is better to get a layer of gold on an adhesive by using single transfer first.

If you wish to share books of gold with friends and colleagues then transfer gold is the sort to buy, as the leaves are easily handled. It is almost impossible to divide a book of loose gold easily without losing at least a couple of leaves. However, remember that you will get a better burnish using loose gold.

Gold, unlike other metals, precious or otherwise, has the facility of sticking to itself, which results in layers of tissue-thin gold leaf building up to form a rich, deep burnish.

All metals need careful handling. A loose leaf of gold, handled

Handle loose gold carefully. Use gold and other metals from the back of the book and bend the back cover away. Allow one leaf with its backing to fall on to a flat surface. Cut the piece of gold you need with a pair of clean scissors. The gold will attach itself to the backing sheet as you cut and can be picked up between your forefinger and thumb nail. If your fingers are greasy, dirty or sweaty the gold will stick to them!

carelessly, will dissolve almost into nothing. Keep the books of gold between pieces of stiff cardboard, or the packing supplied by the shop, until you are ready to use them. Then make sure that you have a clear surface and hold the book flat and with care.

If a leaf of gold falls out of the book do not try to catch it. Instead let it fall and then use a soft paintbrush and a flat, smooth knife to coax it back to where you want it to go. When this happens once, you will realise how careful you have to be in handling loose gold!

Using gold and precious metals

Gold and other precious leaves can be attached to paper or vellum with adhesives such as PVA, gum ammoniac, cryla or acrylic gloss medium, improved gold body, water gold size, gesso, even egg white – or glair – and gelatin (see pages 71 – 73).

Apply the glue or gum, or lay the improved gold body or gesso. Allow to dry if appropriate.

Always use metals from the back of the book; this way you should hold the front leaves carefully and the sheets will not be damaged. If you start from the front then the leaves behind may partially or completely fall from the book and crumple. You can simply remove a leaf of transfer metal and cut what you need from it. For loose metals – bend the back cover away and let the leaves fall on to a flat surface. Carefully separate the last leaf of metal and its backing sheet. Bend the other leaves so that they are held in your hand. Using a pair of good quality new scissors cut a piece of metal of the size you need.

Gold, particularly, will stick to almost anything you do not want it to. If your fingers are greasy or damp the gold leaf will stick to them. Getting the gold to stick to the adhesive is then a problem! To help you handle gold, make a snip along the side of loose gold, through the backing sheet, and the gold should then attach itself to the backing sheet at that point and be easier to handle. Because gold sticks to itself, when you use gold with a snip in it this will not show.

When you are used to handling gold then you can pick it up with your fingertip. It helps if you run your finger through your hair, along your forehead or the side of your nose to pick up some grease.

Burnishing metals

You can lay nine or ten layers of gold to create a good depth of burnish, but only one layer of other metals because they will not stick to themselves.

When all the adhesive in the area you are working on is covered with metal rub over the backing sheet with a burnisher (page 14 – 15), paying particular attention to the edges where getting the gold to stick is sometimes a problem. Remove the backing sheet and replace it with a piece of crystal parchment or glassine. Rub over with the burnisher again. Very gently test the metal with the burnisher directly. If the adhesive is 'calm' then you may burnish the metal directly, and burnish quite hard. If the adhesive is still a little sticky, even with its covering of metal, it is best to leave it for a few hours, or even until the next day, and then burnish.

Gilder's tip, knife and cushion

Gilders who work with a lot of gold at once often use a gilder's cushion. This is a suede covered pad with a protective shield at one end usually made of vellum. It would not be difficult to make one, and not very expensive either.

Armenian bole or French chalk should be sprinkled on the pad of suede. Use the gilder's knife to strop the powder into the cushion. Then scrape away any excess with the knife. This will prevent the gold sticking to the surface of the pad, and make it easier to handle.

As a contrast to illuminatiors using small pieces of gold for manuscripts, gilders, working on large areas such as statues or domes, use whole books of gold at one time. All the 25 leaves of gold are shaken into the end of the cushion, and each leaf then pulled away in turn from the others using the gilder's tip. This is a long, narrow brush, often of squirrel hair, which is run along the nose or through the hair to collect a little grease. The leaf of gold attaches itself to the tip when the brush is gently pressed on it. The gilder's knife is used to cut the squares of gold into smaller pieces.

If you find handling loose gold a problem then a gilder's cushion may be the answer for you. For illuminators one sheet only at a time

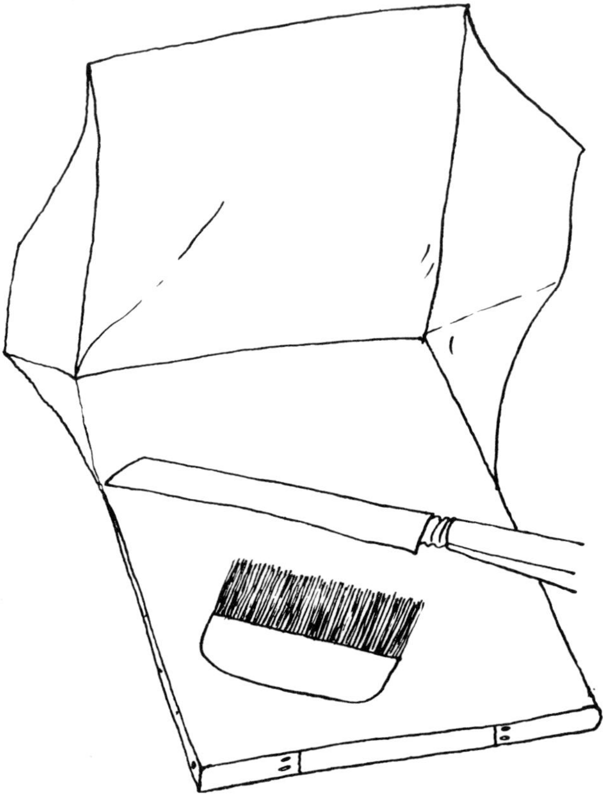

Gilder's knife, tip and cushion.

is pressed on to the cushion. Bend back all the leaves of gold and the cover of the book until only one leaf is showing. Slowly and carefully lower this on to the cushion and press firmly with your fingers. The leaf should stay on the cushion ready for use.

If the leaf is not smooth, lean directly over the cushion with your mouth about 20 – 30cm away. Blow gently and steadily straight on to the gold. If you are at an angle, the leaf of gold will fly away. Do not try to catch it with your fingers, but allow the leaf to settle where it falls. Now slide the knife under the gold leaf and gently lift it back on to the cushion. Handling gold leaf is a technique which you will

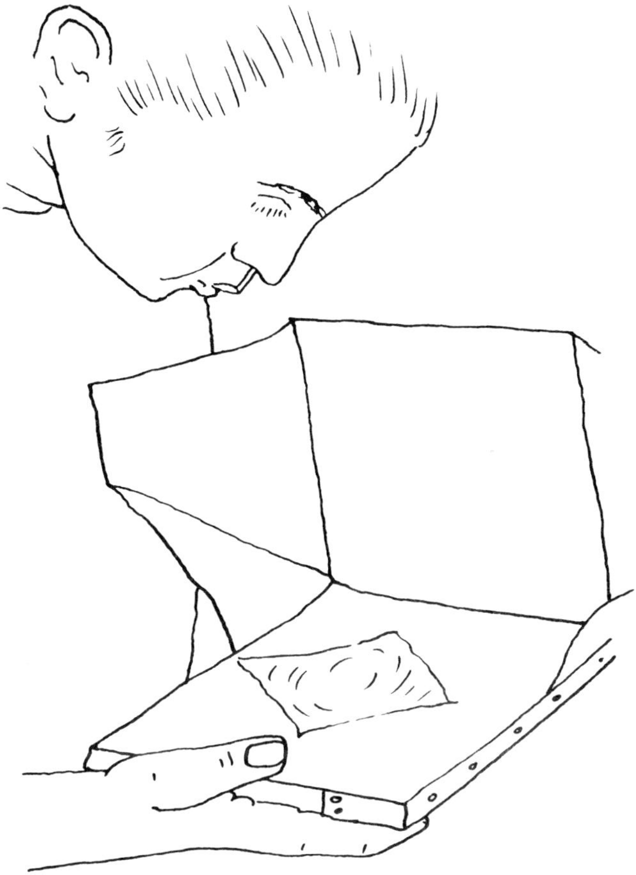

Blowing on the gold to smooth out a crumpled leaf. If you blow at an angle the leaf will fly away. Make sure that your mouth is about 20cm from the surface of the gilder's cushion.

learn slowly at your cost. Most illuminators learn very quickly!

The gilder's knife is then used to 'saw' the leaf into pieces which are the size you want to use. Then pick up the gold using your fingertip and let it gently fall on to the adhesive, or use a gilder's tip which you have run through your hair. Burnish as before.

Gums, Glues and Other Materials

Gold and other metal leaves need some glue or gum to attach them to a surface. Gold in particular does seem to have a mind of its own, and will unfortunately stick to everything and everywhere you do not want it to – scissors, paint surfaces and even your fingers if they are sticky or greasy.

Traditionally only natural glues and gums were used to attach gold, but the advent of modern adhesives has meant that sticking gold and cheaper metals to paper and vellum is more predictable and possibly more permanent. Perhaps it should be noted, though, that the more modern compounds have not stood the test of time. That glair – egg white – attaches gold rather well and does not discolour, affect the gold or migrate from under the gold is proven from the earliest illuminated books, many over 1,000 years old. However, as few of us will be around to see whether our gilded pieces last that long perhaps this should not be too great a consideration!

You may need to experiment a little more with natural, as opposed to synthetic, methods of attaching metal leaf to a surface. The age of an egg and how the chicken is raised will determine how viscous the egg white is, for example, and how much beating will be needed to prevent the liquid becoming stringy. The white of a fresh free range egg is very gelatinous, whereas a three-week-old egg from battery chicken can be almost like water. As well as this the humidity in the atmosphere will affect the stickiness of the glair. On the other hand, manufacturers take great care to ensure that the qualities of modern adhesives are consistent, and do not vary.

Glues – adhesives from animals

Traditionally glues made from bones, skins and other parts of animals have been used as natural adhesives.

Glair – egg white

This is one of the most ancient adhesives for attaching powdered pigment as well as gold. It is mentioned by Pliny (23 – 79AD) and was used by some artists for paintings in Egyptian tombs.

If you have ever tried to remove either dried-on egg white or yolk from a plate or egg cup you will appreciate how effective it is as a glue! The white and yolk should be separated when used with gold, as the white only is used.

How to prepare glair

Crack a fresh egg gently with a knife blade or on the side of a bowl. Allow the white to fall into a large bowl and pass the yolk from half shell to half shell until almost all the white has dropped into the bowl. Put the yolk to one side – it could be used for egg tempera painting, but is not needed for gilding.

Beat the egg white with a fork or an egg whisk until it forms a meringue. It is not necessary for the white to be stiff and in peaks, but there should be froth on top. Beating removes the stringiness of the white.

Allow the egg white to settle for a number of hours, preferably overnight. In the morning pour the liquid which has formed under the froth into a smaller container. This is glair. Discard the froth. Some illuminators prefer to whisk the egg white again, and possibly even a third time, but I have not usually found this necessary.

Powdered or dried egg white can also be bought at most grocers and supermarkets. This does save all the bother of needing fresh eggs, and the smallest quantities can be used, which means you do not have to worry about the glair going off. However, there will be some sort of preservative in the powdered egg white, which may eventually affect your gilding.

How to use

The stickiness of glair is determined by the weather. If it is cold and damp then glair can be used as it is, however, a little water should be added if the atmosphere is dry.

You can write with glair, feeding it into a calligraphy dip pen, or paint it on a surface using a brush.

Using glair does not help rhythm and flow in calligraphy because a layer of leaf gold should be placed over the glair before it dries. This means that you can write only a few letters before stopping to apply the gold leaf. As it is almost waterproof and forms a coating when dry, glair rarely responds then to the moisture from breath.

Once the gold is on the glair place a piece of crystal parchment or glassine paper on the surface and rub over gently with a burnisher. On a test piece, try rubbing over the gold directly.

After a few days, when the glair is completely dry, rub over with a burnisher again to bring up the shine.

Glair as a liquid and glue does not last more than a few days, and it goes bad very quickly if it is covered tightly. To use on the following day place a covering, such as a saucer or even a piece of clingfilm – but do not stretch it tightly over the top, loosely over the glair. Add drops of water to the glair if it dries out.

Vellum size

A sticky size can be made from vellum and/or parchment scraps. Tiny snips of vellum which may be thrown away are ideal for vellum size. Place a handful of vellum scraps in a saucepan and cover with water. Bring to the boil and allow to simmer until only half the liquid remains. Allow to cool. Strain the liquid and scraps through an old nylon tea strainer. Keep the liquid in an airtight jar in the refrigerator. It will set first to a hard jelly and then change into a liquid again. Vellum size can be added to gesso to improve its adhesive properties.

The size will last for about a year, but may grow a mould during that time. Simply skim this off; it will not affect the size. Be warned that vellum size has a particularly powerful smell!

Alternatively, you may prefer to allow the jelly to dry out completely, when it will last indefinitely. Whilst still in jelly form, cut the vellum size into slices, and leave in a clean dry atmosphere for a few days. The vellum size will dry into strips which can be reconstituted with water and used in a similar way to the liquid size. You will need to experiment with the exact amounts of water to add.

Gelatin

Gelatin, similar to glair, was and is used as an adhesive for gold. It is available in granules or sheets from most supermarkets and grocers; the granules are better for gilding.

Gelatin should be dissolved in hot, not boiling, water and it is always best to add the granules to the water and stir briskly, rather than adding water to granules. For gilding, add water in a proportion of 4:1, that is, four parts water to one of granules. A little goes a very long way, so you will not need to make a lot of the solution.

Paint or write with gelatin in a similar way to glair. You should place the gold leaf over the gelatin whilst it is still liquid, before it sets. This does not aid your rhythm and flow if you are using gelatin for lettering.

Place a piece of crystal parchment or glassine over the gold and rub very gently with a burnisher. You may be able to burnish again a few days later when the gelatin has set, but it remains rather fragile even then.

Once it is cold gelatin sets into a solid jelly. This may happen while you are using it. If so, simply warm the gelatin by placing the container in a bowl of hot water and allow the heat from the water to change the jelly back into a liquid again.

Seccotine or fish glue

Seccotine or fish glue is used as one of the sticky substances in gesso and is not used on its own by calligraphers. It is liquid when cold and is used full strength. Hide and bone glues are stronger, but they are normally used hot. See pages 84 – 85 for making gesso.

Gums – adhesives from trees and plants

Most of these gums are traditional but not all are used for gilding.

Gum ammoniac

This is usually sold both as a liquid and in rubbery lumps. It is more economical to buy lumps as you can then make small amounts of the liquid when you require it; the stickiness in the liquid is not everlasting. On the other hand it is convenient to buy a jar of already prepared solution.

How to make liquid gum ammoniac
The lumps do last a very long time and making a solution is not difficult. Simply put a few lumps – break up any of the larger ones – into a small jar and cover with water. Tilt the jar on a pencil or the edge of your palette so that it is at an angle and leave overnight. In the morning there will be a milky liquid. Stir again and then strain through an old nylon tea strainer into another jar. Do not push the dregs through the mesh otherwise it will spoil the liquid.

Add a drop of food colouring to the liquid as this will help you see where you have written or painted.

You can use gum ammoniac for lettering and painting, although you should wash your brush frequently and wash out your pen carefully, as the liquid will set hard.

When the gum ammoniac solution is dry, which may take from twenty minutes to two hours, you can start to gild. Cover everything but a small area of lettering or painted gum ammoniac with pieces of crystal parchment. With your mouth about 5cm from the paper or vellum breathe out one long slow breath. Immediately place a piece of gold over the gum and press down firmly with your fingers. Remove the backing sheet if you have used transfer gold or metal and place a piece of crystal parchment or glassine over the gold. Rub over gently with a burnisher. Repeat this process over the whole area to be gilded. The next day, gently test an area of gold. Sometimes you may be able to burnish directly over the gold, but be aware that too much heat will distort the gum ammoniac and the leaf gold will lose its purchase. It may be better to burnish only with the crystal parchment.

You can write quite fine letters with gum ammoniac and it is one of the preferred media for gilded calligraphy.

If you have problems in attaching the gold it may be that there is simply not enough gum ammoniac on the paper or vellum. This could happen particularly on the finer strokes of letters. To avoid this problem, when writing the thinnest parts of the letters, press your pen nib to increase the flow of liquid before you make the thinner stroke.

Gum arabic

Gum arabic, obtained naturally from certain species of tropical *acacia,* is rarely used for gilding. Although it is possible to attach leaf gold to painted gum arabic it is rarely used because other media are easier and more successful.

Usually drops of gum arabic are added to paints to improve their adherence to paper and vellum. If you have left paint in a palette for a number of weeks and it has dried, some of the gum may have evaporated with the water. Add more water to the dried out paint to make a liquid again and test a little of it. Allow it to dry. Rub over with your finger. If the paint can be brushed off easily, add a couple of drops of gum arabic to the mix and try again.

When using coloured paints for writing or painting in a manuscript book it is worth adding drops of gum arabic anyway to the paint, especially red and blue, as both colours easily transfer. This helps to alleviate 'off-set', where the paint comes off on the opposite page.

Gum arabic can also be mixed with bronze powders so that they adhere to paper.

To make gum arabic from lump form

Grind the lumps of gum arabic with a pestle and mortar until they form a fine powder. Wash the pestle and mortar carefully and thoroughly.

In a proportion of 2:1, water to powder, add the gum arabic powder to distilled boiling water and stir slowly. Allow the solution to stand for 24 hours, and then pour the liquid into an airtight jar, leaving behind any residue.

Gum sandarac

The yellow hard crystals of gum sandarac, from the coniferous plant *Callitris quadrivalvis,* are used by artists to make varnish. Scribes use gum sandarac in a different way. The lumps of gum, slightly dusty on the surface, have to be ground before they can be used. Put about a 5ml spoonful, or a teaspoonful, into a clean mortar. Grind until a pale yellow powder is formed. Tip the powder into an airtight jar, and label it. Wash the pestle and mortar as soon as you have tipped out the powder otherwise the powder will set solid into a gum in the pestle and be very difficult to remove at a later stage.

Gum sandarac is used as a resist for lettering. It shrinks the ink very slightly so that letterstrokes are crisp and fine. The powder can be applied to both paper and vellum.

Either sprinkle a little over the paper or vellum and rub in gently or tip some powder into a 10cm (4 inches) square of finely woven cotton, such as an old handkerchief or a piece of cotton sheeting. Gather up the edges and wind a piece of string around so that you have a small bag or pad. Dab this over the area where you will be writing. You do not need a great amount; too much will act so much as a resist such that the letters will have two separate strokes with nothing in the centre, and you will have to either rewrite it, or go over these letters with a fine brush.

Before you write, go over the paper or vellum with a very soft brush to remove any excess powder. This can be reused, so brush it on to a piece of scrap paper and tip the powder back into the storage jar.

Synthetic adhesives

Modern adhesives are easy to use, need very little preparation and certainly make gold stick. However, some have their drawbacks, too.

Cryla gloss medium, acrylic gloss medium, PVA

These can be used for gilding as well as in their more usual form in acrylic painting. They are very sticky and will certainly make the gold stick, but they do not sit particularly flat on a surface. The medium will often 'blob' through a pen and you can see the individual brush marks when the medium is laid with a brush. Diluting with water 50:50 does help, but then you will need to add an additional layer or two, as the first will soak into the paper. Although this is not too much of a problem with painting, going exactly over letters written with a pen is not easy and may well ruin the sharpness and liveliness of the lettering.

Always wash your brush and pen immediately after using as the medium will set hard. If possible, use an old brush to save potentially spoiling good brushes.

How to use

Paint or letter with the gloss medium or PVA, and allow it to dry. Cut a piece of gold of the size you need. With your mouth about 5cm from the paper, breathe long and slowly and immediately place the gold over the acrylic gloss or cryla gloss medium. Press firmly all over with your fingers. Remove the backing sheet and replace with crystal parchment or glassine. Rub over with a burnisher paying particular attention to the edges. When the medium is 'calm' then you can rub over the gold directly with the burnisher. Allow it to settle for a few minutes and test a small area. If there is any stickiness then give it longer to dry.

You can add extra layers of gold for a deeper burnish.

Gilding Medium

This is a liquid especially manufactured for use in illuminating. It usually contains PVA and other substances to make the gold stick. For some reason or other gilding medium is usually a rather bright shade of pink!

Gilding medium works well when used for painting areas with a brush for gilding, but not all makes are good for lettering with a pen, so, if you can, do have a trial run with an offcut first.

Use an old brush for painting with gilding medium as the PVA content ruins good brushes. Wash your pen out carefully after use, too.

How to use

Paint or letter with the medium. Allow it to dry, which often takes only about 10 minutes. With your mouth about 5cm from the applied medium breathe to reactivate the stickiness and apply the gold. Cover with crystal parchment paper and rub over with a burnisher. When the medium is 'calm' you can burnish directly over the gold. Apply more than one layer of gold for a deeper burnish.

Water gold size

Water gold size is a bright yellow fairly viscous liquid. It works well with gold when it is applied with a brush, but does not flow particularly well through a pen. The liquid is a little too thick for a nib, and the letters are uneven and a little blobby. Diluting the gold size can sometimes improve on this.

How to use

Stir the water gold size gently with the end of a paintbrush. A vigorous shake will introduce air bubbles, which you should try to avoid. Paint over the area to be gilded with a brush. Allow to dry, which may take between 10 to 20 minutes. While it is still tacky apply the gold and burnish as before. If the gold size dries out too much then its stickiness can be reactivated by breathing directly over the applied medium.

Improved gold body

This thick yellow mix is used by some illuminators as a substitute for gesso. Its viscosity means that it makes a raised cushion when it dries. However it is often difficult to get the gold to stick round the edges, and you may be left with a yellow border around the gold.

This is not a problem if you then edge the gold with paint, as was done in traditional manuscript painting. The ingredients of improved gold body are such that the gold sticks well to the compound, which is not always the case with gesso! However, the brightness of the burnish is not so great with improved gold body.

Before use stir carefully with the end of a paintbrush. Do not shake or stir vigorously as this will introduce air bubbles which take a very long time to disperse.

How to use

Apply the gold body with a paintbrush. As it is so sticky and thick it does not pass through a pen well, even when diluted. Allow to dry and apply layers of gold as before.

Go round the outline of the gold with a fine brush and paint, or a quill and ink if you prefer the edge to be neat and sharp.

Writer's gold size, Japan gold size

Both these mixes are manufactured specifically for gilders and sign writers who work in wood, stone and glass, rather than illuminators who work on paper and vellum. These sizes are oil based and so should not be applied to paper or vellum as the oil will spread and ruin your work. Illuminators should leave these in the shop!

Other materials

Scribes and illuminators do use other materials in their work; although none is essential, they can make life a little easier.

Masking fluid or rubber solution

Masking fluid is a rubbery solution which you can use with a pen or brush, but both will need frequent washing. Apply the solution to the area or letters where you want to retain the colour of the paper or the colour of a wash which you have already laid. Allow to dry. Paint over with another colour or wash – watercolour or dilute gouache are both ideal. Allow these to dry and then remove the masking fluid with a clean finger or eraser. You can add more areas or masking fluid lettering with additional washes, as you wish.

Sometimes the masking fluid is very sticky and catches in the pen nib. If this is a problem dilute the fluid with a few drops of water – too much and the masking fluid will not act as a resist.

Armenian bole and dragon's blood

This red earth colour of Armenian bole owes its hue to iron oxide. It is sold as a powder or in lump form which then needs to be ground with a pestle and mortar. This bole is used to colour gesso, and is why that is usually a pale pink.

Armenian bole can also be used to make a 'carbon paper' for transferring designs and patterns without the use of graphite. Use A4 sheets of thin bond paper, such as photocopying paper. Place a sheet of this on some old newspaper and sprinkle only a very little Armenian bole powder over the copying paper. With a clean pad of cotton wool, rub the powder into the paper. Try to get an even coating over the surface. With a clean piece of cotton wool, wipe off the excess powder. Store the paper between a folded A3 piece of photo-copying paper or in a transparent plastic wallet to avoid mess.

When you have traced a design on tracing paper to transfer on to paper or vellum, position it where it is to be and attach it to the surface with a couple of tiny pieces of masking tape. Slide the Armenian bole paper face down between the tracing paper and the surface. Go over the outline with a blunt point, such as a ball point pen which has run out, or perhaps with a hard, say 4H, pencil.

The design will be transferred to the paper or vellum and you will have no graphite which may be difficult to remove from the surface. Go over your design using a fine brush and very dilute red ochre gouache, to be in keeping with traditional manuscript painting.

When the paint has dried, remove the original Armenian bole line with a soft eraser. You will have your design then ready to paint.

Armenian bole is sometimes confused with dragon's blood. Dragon's blood is in fact a transparent resin and not a true pigment, although it was used as one from Roman times. Pliny explains the source of dragon's blood as being produced as a result of the deaths of a dragon and an elephant. Thick matter from the dead dragon mixed with blood from the two animals to make dragon's blood. In fact dragon's blood comes from an Asiatic tree. Pliny felt that it was the only colour which could truly represent the colour of blood.

Crocus Powder

Crocus powder is also a red colour and is slightly abrasive, similar to jeweller's rouge. It is used to very slightly roughen or add tooth to polished metal burnishers, such as hæmatite and psilomelanite.

It is best to make your own crocus cloth from the powder, using a small piece, about 10cm or 4 inches square, of finely woven cotton, perhaps an old handkerchief or a piece of cotton sheeting.

Sprinkle some crocus powder on the material and rub over with your fingers. Push the powder into the material as much as you can. When the cloth is quite red in colour shake off the excess which can be returned to the storage jar.

With the burnisher held in one hand, rub the shiny metal end for about 30 seconds or a minute with the crocus cloth which is held in the other hand.

French Chalk

The slippery properties of this magnesium silicate powder are used in gilding. The procedure of gilding is that, when there is gold and painting together, all work with gold is done first, to avoid the gold attaching itself to the gum in the paint. Occasionally there are times when this is not possible and painting has to be done before the gilding. In this instance, the paint is brushed with a small amount of French chalk powder, and this helps to prevent the gold sticking to the paint. After gilding the white powder is removed by brisk brushing and the excess returned to the storage jar.

It can also be used to make white 'carbon' paper, in a similar way to Armenian bole paper on page 80.

Gilder's Whiting

Gilder's whiting is natural calcium carbonate which has been ground and washed. It is used to provide bulk when mixed with paints. Paris white is the best grade; lower grades make putty when mixed with oil.

Gilder's whiting can also be used to make gesso, substituting for the slaked plaster of Paris. Although chemically there seems to be no reason why there should be any problem with this, the shine of gold on gesso made with gilder's whiting is not, in my experience, so great as on that made with slaked plaster of Paris. However, there are sometimes problems in obtaining the plaster, and so gilder's whiting may be the best substitute in these instances.

Plaster of Paris

Slaked plaster of Paris is used as the main ingredient to make gesso, which is the bulking compound for illumination. In mediæval manuscript books, layers of leaf gold sit on a slightly raised smooth cushion of gesso, and this looks as if the whole of that part is of solid gold.

Calcium carbonate is heated until it loses three-quarters of its water; this makes plaster of Paris. It has to be slaked so that it becomes inert. This can be done in two ways. Usually it is mixed to a thick creamy paste and used to make moulds. Heat is generated in this reaction and the paste sets to a solid within about 10 minutes. Because it sets more quickly than the water can evaporate, there is no decrease in its bulk; for this reason it is used by dentists and others who need to take an accurate mould.

The second method of slaking plaster of Paris is to use a large quantity of water and a lot of stirring. The heat is lost in the volume of water and rather than setting to a mould, the plaster remains a powder, which is eventually made inert by constant changes of water. This is the method used by illuminators.

How to slake plaster of Paris

There are two methods, one traditional and slow, and the other modern and a lot quicker!

THE TRADITIONAL METHOD You will need large quantities of distilled water, a large 10 litre or 2 gallon bucket, a plastic spoon for stirring and about 500g or 1lb of plaster of Paris powder.

Fill the bucket to the top with distilled water and gently sprinkle the powder into the water, stirring steadily all the time. If you add the water to the powder, or if you do not stir, the plaster will set solid.

Stir for at least 30 minutes – preferably an hour. Allow the plaster to settle at the bottom of the bucket. Gently pour the water off the top, keeping as much plaster in the bucket as you can.

Fill the bucket to the top with water again and stir for 10 minutes.

Allow the water to stand overnight. Tip away the water, reserving the plaster, fill to the top and stir again for ten minutes. Allow the water to stand overnight. Repeat this every day for seven days and then every other day for fourteen days. After this the plaster will be slaked.

Now tip the water away for the last time. The plaster can be allowed to stand in the bottom of the bucket until all the water has evaporated, and will then need to be scraped away from the container. You may prefer to strain the sloppy mix remaining in the bucket through folded muslin or an old tea towel or pillowcase to retain the plaster. It can then be allowed to dry out in one lump or in a few smaller ones.

When completely dry store away from anywhere which contains iron, as this will discolour it. A large screw top airtight glass jar is a good container for slaked plaster of Paris.

A QUICKER METHOD The plaster which was available in mediæval times was not very pure, and the washings of water cleared away a lot of the impurities. The washings in distilled water change the calcium carbonate from alkali to a neutral mix, that is, a pH of 7.

For this modern method you will need a large glass mixing bowl, a plastic spoon for stirring and again quantities of distilled water, but you do not have to wait so long. You will also need some means of testing the acidity/alkalinity, or pH, of the liquid. Litmus paper, Universal Indicator or even a soil or swimming pool testing kit are all ideal.

Fill the large mixing bowl with distilled water and use a smaller quantity of plaster of Paris, about 100g or 4oz. Sprinkle the plaster on the water and stir all the time. Do not allow the plaster to settle, stirring for at least 15 minutes.

Now allow the plaster to settle and pour away the water. Fill to the top quickly with distilled water and stir again for 10 minutes. Repeat this nine or ten times.

It may take a couple of hours as you have to allow the plaster a reasonable time to settle, otherwise you will lose more plaster than you keep when you pour away the water.

The difference between the traditional and more modern methods comes now. Test the water at this point. If it does not have a pH of 7 then repeat the washings and pouring away of the water until it does.

Once the water is neutral the plaster has been slaked. Pour off the excess water and allow it to dry as before.

Gesso

Gesso forms the slightly raised cushion which supports layers of leaf gold and raises them from the surface of paper or vellum. Occasionally you can buy ready-made gesso from specialist suppliers, and some people have had good results for illuminating using this. However, as gold is so expensive, you may prefer to make your own gesso so that you can control the ingredients and how it is made. The finer the gesso the better your gilding will be.

To make gesso

There are five ingredients for gesso. Slaked plaster of Paris provides the bulk. Lead carbonate – **which is poisonous and should be**

handled very carefully, use gloves and a mask if you prefer – fills in any of the spaces between the plaster particles, provides bulk and also acts as a fungicide. Glue and sugar attract the moisture from your breath and makes the gesso sticky so that the gold will adhere to it. Armenian bole provides colour.

The recipe for gesso is:

8 parts of powdered slaked plaster of Paris
**3 parts of lead carbonate*
1 part of sugar (some prefer sugar candy or preserving sugar)
1 part of glue, usually this is seccotine or fish glue
a pinch of Armenian bole
***This is poisonous and should be handled very carefully**

The parts can be any measurement although usually a tiny salt spoon or very small coffee spoon (less than 3ml) is sufficient. Count out the required quantities of plaster, lead and sugar on to a sheet of smooth paper – this should avoid errors in your counting. Tip the powders into a pestle and add a pinch of Armenian bole for colour. Grind carefully for 20 minutes. Note that this is grinding and not simply stirring. You should have a fine pale pink powder.

Now add the glue using the same spoon for measuring. Scrape as much of the glue from the spoon as you can. Add distilled water to the mix over the spoon, so that as much glue is washed off as possible. Stir round with the mortar so that the result is a thin paste. Now continue grinding for another 10 minutes, frequently scraping the pink paste from the sides of the pestle.

Put small dabs, no more than 1cm in diameter, on to a piece of foil, and allow to dry out in a clean atmosphere. The gesso is best left to dry before using, although once dried it can be used straight away. Store the dried gesso in an airtight container and it will last for many years.

Reconstituting gesso

Peel one or two of the small dabs of gesso away from the foil and put them into a small glass jar. Tilt the jar on its side by resting it on a pencil or the side of your palette. Add two drops of distilled water. Leave for a couple of hours.

The water will soak into the gesso and slightly soften it. Add more water, drop by drop and stir very gently with the end of a paintbrush until the gesso is the consistency of thin, runny cream. Do take care at this stage. You want to avoid bubbles in gesso, so do not stir vigorously, nor more than you have to.

If there are bubbles in the gesso, dip the end of your paintbrush in oil of cloves (from a chemist or pharmacy) and stir the gesso with that. (Oil of cloves is used to alleviate tooth ache. If you do not clean the end of the paintbrush then the oil of cloves will be contaminated by the lead carbonate from the gesso, and so should certainly not be used for toothache afterwards!)

Using gesso

Gesso can be laid on paper or vellum using a brush or pen. It is better to use a quill with a slightly longer slit if you have the choice. The action of passing through the quill seems to help prevent air bubbles.

There is a technique to laying gesso. Stir the gesso gently to make sure that there is an even mix of all the constituents. Scoop a little of the gesso with the brush or pen. Press the brush or pen down on to the paper or vellum to release the liquid and then work the gesso around the intended letter or shape. You can write calligraphic or expressive letters with gesso, and cover quite large areas with a surprisingly small amount.

Do not allow the edge of gesso to dry out, it is a 'wet-in-wet' process, in that you should move carefully around an area if you are painting, continually working at the edge of the wet gesso. You can 'blob' more gesso on to that which has already been laid to make it higher as long as it is still wet.

It is possible to add additional layers of gesso to build up the level, but the first layer should be allowed to dry overnight. Paint this with water and a brush to slightly soften the surface and give a slight 'key', and then add another thin layer of gesso.

Allow the gesso to dry, preferably overnight or longer. Sometimes the gesso may look dry on the surface, but be quite soft underneath. You may find this out only when you burnish hard and the gesso crumbles under the layers of gold leaf.

Preparing gesso for gilding

When you are sure the gesso is quite dry the surface should be prepared. Attach your vellum or paper to a smooth hard surface, if you have not done this before. The best surface is a piece of plate glass (about 15cm, or 12 inches, square), where the edges have been ground and then covered with strong tape for safety. A smooth hard surface is essential as you exert some pressure when doing the final burnish. If the underlying layer is at all compliant the gesso may crack. In addition the cold, smooth surface of glass is best for condensing the moisture of your breath on the gesso surface.

The better the surface of gesso is, the better will be your final gilding. Having worked with gold for many years and tried various methods, I now recommend scraping the surface of the gesso first. With a curved-bladed knife, gently scrape the surface so that any bumps or dips are evened out. The surface should be very slightly cushioned. Avoid a plateau effect, with very steep sides and a flat top.

When you are satisfied that it is as smooth as you can make it, rub over the surface with an agate burnisher (see page 15) or with a very smooth, polished stone. You want to polish the gesso so that it shines.

Both these processes ensure that the surface is as good as you can make it before the gold is laid.

Laying gold leaf

You will need leaves of both single and double gold to create a depth of burnish. If you are not experienced, then use *single transfer* and *double loose* leaves of gold. Other items of equipment you will require are a burnisher (see page 14 – 15), a pair of new and good quality small craft scissors, a small piece of silk and small pieces of crystal parch-ment paper or glassine.

Breathe on your burnisher and rub over the polished end with the piece of silk. This cleans and polishes it.

Mask off everything but a small area of gesso with pieces of crystal parchment paper. Have everything that you need to hand before you start. The key to gilding is speed and breathing. There are about three seconds between your breathing and the gold sticking. This does not allow time for you to cut and pick up the gold, finding your burnisher and so on.

Cut a piece of single gold leaf (transfer possibly) which easily covers the area which is not masked. Hold this in one hand with your burnisher and a piece of crystal parchment within easy reach.

Lean over the gesso so that your mouth is about 5cm away and make two very long hard breaths. The air from the bottom of your lungs contains the most moisture so make sure you empty your lungs with air each time. Immediately place the gold over the sticky gesso and press down firmly all over with your fingers. Go over the gold with a burnisher, paying particular attention to the edges.

Remove the backing sheet and replace it with a piece of crystal parchment. Rub over with the burnisher again.

Cut another piece of single gold and breathe over the gesso once again. Place the gold immediately on the surface and repeat the previous operation. Now use pieces of double loose gold. Loose gold moulds itself much better over the gesso but is more difficult to handle. Look back at pages 65 and 66 for this. Cut a piece of double gold and place over the single gold already sticking to the gesso. Rub over with a burnisher, remove the backing sheet, replace with crystal parchment and rub over again.

Some gold may be surrounding the gesso which could be used. Slide a knife under this and turn it over on to the gesso. Rub over with a burnisher.

Try to build up a depth of layers of gold. At some point the gold will stick to itself rather than the gesso, so perhaps it is best to stop at about eight layers, although nine or ten will look really stunning!

Now rub over the gold directly with the burnisher. The gesso may be a little soft from the moisture in your breath, so test it carefully. When it is 'calm' you can rub over the gold very hard with the burnisher. Burnishing is not tickling. Having a hard backing surface should mean that the gesso does not crack under the strain. You should have a mirror shine on the gold that you can see your face in.

Leave the gold overnight, and you can burnish it again. It is also a good idea, if you are framing your work, to burnish again just prior to framing.

Cleaning around the gold and finishing off

When you have finished gilding and burnishing there may be some pieces of gold stuck to the paper or vellum around the gesso.

These can be removed in two ways. The traditional way is to use the blade of a very sharp knife and gently scratch away the excess gold. Or you may prefer to use a hard eraser, a typist's eraser – the sort sold as a pencil, which can then be sharpened to a point – is best. Gently rub away the gold, taking particular care not to rub too near the brightly shining gold as the abrasive quality of the eraser will actually remove the gold leaf.

In mediæval manuscripts the raised gold was usually outlined in black. This is best done with a quill rather than a brush, as the sharp quill 'bites' into the gold and gives the paint or ink a purchase. A fine brush simply washes over the gold. You can also outline your shiny raised gold with shell gold if you prefer, so that there is not a hard outline of black against the gold.

When all this is done you can complete your painting around the burnished gold, perhaps using egg tempera, see pages 52 – 58.

Ox gall liquid

Ox gall is a wetting agent; it reduces surface tension in a liquid. It is useful to add to paints which may be a little sticky so that they become smooth and silky when used. It should not be confused with oak galls, which are used to make ink, see page 33. Similar to some other products used in calligraphy, ox gall liquid smells pretty awful!

Pounce and pumice

Some papers and surfaces of vellum are ideal for calligraphy; some need a little coaxing to create beautifully sharp letters, with crisp outlines. Pounce is ideal for this as it removes any grease from the surface and also creates a little 'tooth', which allows the pen to bite into the paper or vellum. Pounce is particularly good for papers where the pen skids over the surface and does not have any grip.

Pounce is a mixture of ground pumice powder and ground cuttlefish powder. It is mixed in a ratio of 2:1, pumice to cuttlefish. Pumice powder is usually available from specialist suppliers, or from chemists or pharmacists. Cuttlefish bone can be picked up from most beaches (it will need to be washed and cleaned with water, and then left to dry), or is available from petshops. Budgerigars like cuttlefish, too!

If the pumice or cuttlefish are still in lump form you will need to first break them down into smaller lumps. The best way of doing this is to wrap them separately in layers of old newspaper and hit them with a hammer on a hard surface outside. This breaks the large lumps much smaller ones or into powder. Now grind the lumps and powder, again separately, with a pestle and mortar so that they form a fine powder.

Tip the powder on to a piece of smooth paper. Now combine the powders in the ratio of two parts of pumice powder to one part of cuttlefish powder. Pounce is almost everlasting so it is best to use up all the powder you have made, as long as the proportions are consistent. Tip the mix into a screw top, airtight jar and label.

To use pounce you can make a little pounce bag similar to that for gum sandarac powder, see page 76, or you may prefer to use it directly. Before you start, place a sheet of scrap paper folded in half underneath your paper or vellum say A3 folded to A4 size. Tip some pounce powder on to the best paper or vellum, about 10ml or a tablespoonful. With another small piece of paper, a small scrap of vellum, a piece of cotton wool, or even your fingers, gently rub all over the surface in a systematic way with the pounce.

When you have finished, carefully lift the sheet of best paper or vellum and tip all the pounce on to the folded piece of scrap paper. With a soft brush clean the pounce from the surface. The folded scrap paper can now be used to transfer the excess pounce back into the storage jar so that it can be used again.

Alternatively, you can go over the surface with the pounce bag, gently rolling it all over the paper or vellum. Again remove the excess with a soft brush.

If there is a gritty feeling on the paper, or if pounce collects in your pen nib, then you should dust the pounce from the paper again as you have left too much on the surface.

Index

Main entry shown in **bold type**

Further Reading

Cennini, d'Andrea Cennino, *Il Libro dell'Arte, The Craftsman's Handbook),* translated by Daniel V Thompson, Dover, 1960
Gettens and Stout, *Painting Materials – A Short Encyclopædia,* Dover, 1966
Lovett, Patricia, *Calligraphy for Starters,* Images, 1995
Lovett, Patricia, *Calligraphy for Starters* – video, Cable Crouch Productions/Watchword Educational Library, 1995
Lovett, Patricia, *Teach Yourself Calligraphy,* Hodder and Stoughton, 1993
Mayer, Ralph, *The Artist's Handbook of Materials and Techniques,* Faber and Faber, 1987
Sassoon and Lovett, *Creating Letterforms,* Thames and Hudson, 1992
Thompson, Daniel V, *The Practice of Tempera Painting,* Dover, 1962
Wilcox, Michael, *Blue and Yellow Don't Make Green,* Collins, 1989

Societies

Calligraphy and Lettering Arts Society, 54 Boileau Road, London SW13 9BL
L E T T E R S, Hernewood, Gracious Lane, Sevenoaks, Kent TN13 1TJ
Society of Scribes and Illuminators, 6 Queen Square, London WC1N 3AR